Governing Britain since 1945

Governing Britain since 1945

Nigel Knight

POLITICO'S

First published in Great Britain 2006 by
Politico's Publishing Ltd, an imprint of
Methuen Publishing Ltd
11–12 Buckingham Gate
London
SW1E 6LB

10 9 8 7 6 5 4 3 2 1

Copyright © Nigel Knight 2006.

Nigel Knight has asserted his right under the Copyright, Designs and Patents Act 1988
to be identified as the author of this work.

A CIP catalogue record for this book is available from the British Library.

ISBN-10: 1-84275-178-6
ISBN-13: 978-1-84275-178-7

Typeset by SX Composing DTP, Rayleigh, Essex
Printed and bound in Great Britain by The Cromwell Press, Trowbridge, Wiltshire

To Vic, Joy, Ernie, Iris and Sally

Contents

Preface and acknowledgements

Since 1945 Britain has been transformed from a global imperial power into a medium-sized European state. In *Governing Britain since 1945* I cast a quizzical eye over the governments, policies and politicians that have managed and attempted to reverse this decline. The transformation has been largely contrary to government policy: governments of both political parties were initially resistant both to the process of dismantling the empire and particularly to adjusting to the fact that Britain was patently no longer a hegemonic power. For years after the Second World War, both the British people and the British establishment were subject to an 'illusion of grandeur'. In 1945 Britain's place in the world was perhaps summed up best by Winston Churchill's notion of 'three spheres of influence', viz. the USA, Europe and Britain with its empire, intersecting like a Venn diagram. Britain was still seen as having a similar status to the US. In reality Britain's status had already diminished in relation to the US even before 1945, and subsequently, the development of European unification would lessen it further.

During much of the post-war period successive governments and the civil service were responsible for managing Britain's relative economic, and absolute strategic, decline. To some extent the system of governance has only partially kept pace with this change. Britain has been, and to some extent remains, over-governed in terms of the total numerical size of the administrative system, and the attitudes and policies of politicians have to some extent lagged behind the diminishing status of a once great power.

Although Britain was subject to a decline in status globally, there was nevertheless a gradual improvement in the day-to-day lives of most British people, and this improvement has accelerated for most since the 1980s. In 1945 Britain still had an 'empire upon which the sun never set', but there was widespread poverty and social deprivation: sixty years later both of these have largely gone. Social policy was transformed after the Second World War and remains a central feature of Britain today: social security, the provision of health care and education, and housing were revolutionised in the immediate post-war years.

The transformation of Britain from an imperial power to a member of the European Union, although highly reliant upon the USA for defence and foreign policy issues, has been and remains fraught. The real problem is that sixty years is a short period of time: no one in Italy or Greece or Egypt believes that their nation currently enjoys a status commensurate with that of their dominant position in antiquity, but this is because so much time has elapsed since that dominance. Britain desires the independence to act as it once did, still within living memory, but in reality it has become highly dependent upon both the USA and Europe.

The book offers a highly accessible and readable account. Specifically, *Governing Britain since 1945* provides a summary of the Prime Ministers and their governments and policies; it also gives an exposition of the system of national governance and of local and regional government.

I would like to acknowledge all the staff and students at the University of Cambridge who have been helpful to me, but especially Professor William Brown and Dr Kanak Patel for their unstinting support. Also Alan Gordon Walker and Jonathan Wadman at Politico's have offered exceptional help. But most of all I would like to thank Sally Goodsell, without whom this book would not have come about.

Nigel Knight
Cambridge, July 2006

1

Summary: the Prime Ministers, their governments and policies

The function of this summary is to enable readers to navigate their way around post-war British governments, and their principal ideas and policies. This period was composed of governments formed by two parties, Labour and Conservative, and there were two periods of broad consensus between the parties on policy while in government, one prior to 1979 and one after it. What follows is a brief exposition of each Prime Minister, their period(s) in office and their governments' achievements.

1945–51 Clement Attlee (Labour)

Clement Attlee became Labour Prime Minister in a landslide election victory in the summer of 1945, having been deputy Prime Minister under Winston Churchill in the war-time coalition government. The Attlee government would be a radical one, implementing the welfare state polices laid down by William Beveridge's 1942 report. The policies would include the creation of the National Health Service, the implementation of R. A. Butler's 1944 Education Act, the nationalisation of some principal industries and the introduction of Keynesian demand management policies to maintain full employment. However, foreign, colonial and defence policy would not change appreciably, and the British atomic bomb project was initiated. This government would lay the foundations of the post-war consensus. The Attlee government narrowly won the 1950 general election but another one was called a year later because of the small majority; however, as the government had largely run out of ideas, it lost.

1951–5 Winston Churchill (Conservative)

Winston Churchill would return as Conservative Prime Minister in the general election of 1951, having been Prime Minister in the coalition government during the Second World War. The radical leftward shift in public opinion by the end of the war meant that Churchill, having opposed the Labour manifesto in 1945, was now, through political pragmatism, obliged broadly to adopt it. His government would thus keep the welfare state essentially intact. However, it did denationalise the iron and steel industry and road freight transport. He completed the Labour government programme to produce the atomic bomb, and attempted to reinvigorate the Anglo-American alliance that had been so important during the war. However, Britain had been eclipsed as a superpower and so was increasingly marginalised by the USA. Churchill suffered two strokes, in 1949 and 1953, which were concealed from the public. His Cabinet forced him to retire in the spring of 1955 at the advanced age of eighty.

1955–7 Anthony Eden (Conservative)

Anthony Eden, who had been 'heir apparent' to Winston Churchill, replaced him on Churchill's retirement in 1955. Eden immediately held a general election, which increased the Conservative majority. He had enormous experience in foreign affairs, having been Foreign Secretary during the war, and for a period before it, as well as in Churchill's post-war government. Despite this he was responsible for the catastrophe of the Suez crisis in 1956, where Britain's attempt to regain the Suez canal by force after its nationalisation by Egypt was thwarted by the USA for fear of the USSR's reaction. Given this, and with ill health dogging him, he paid with his job in January of the following year.

1957–63 Harold Macmillan (Conservative)

Harold Macmillan, who had been Chancellor of the Exchequer, replaced Anthony Eden as Prime Minister and presided over the completion of the post-war economic recovery, and as a consequence his government won the 1959 general election. The consensus on economic and social policy continued. Macmillan initiated the decolonialisation policy and applied for membership of the European Economic Community (EEC), though this was rejected by the French. He negotiated the purchase of Polaris submarine-launched nuclear missiles from President Kennedy. The Profumo scandal, concerning the Secretary of State for War, John Profumo, a prostitute and a Soviet spy, and the 'night of the long knives' when he fired a third of his Cabinet, collectively proved to be the beginning of the end for him as Prime Minister. Ill health finally caused him to resign in 1963.

1963–4 Alec Douglas-Home (Conservative)

Alec Douglas-Home (pronounced 'Hume') replaced Harold Macmillan in 1963, having been Foreign Secretary in Macmillan's government. He lasted a year as Prime Minister until the general election in 1964, when he professed to know nothing about economics, while his Labour adversary professed to know a great deal. He consequently lost. He did, however, return as Foreign Secretary for a further period in Edward Heath's government in the 1970s.

1964–70 Harold Wilson (Labour)

Harold Wilson became Labour Prime Minister in the 1964 general election after thirteen years of continuous Conservative rule. Wilson had replaced Hugh Gaitskell as Labour Party leader after Gaitskell's untimely death, and he promised to transform the British economy in the 'white heat of technology'. It had been clear for some time that the British economy had not been as productive as those of the USA and West Germany, but Wilson's government planning failed to rectify this. He was, however, a skilful politician, and managed to increase Labour's majority in a general election in 1966. Having devalued the pound in 1967 and applied for EEC membership, which was again rejected, and having had to move troops into Northern Ireland in 1969, he lost the 1970 general election.

1970–4 Edward Heath (Conservative)

Edward Heath, who in 1965 had become the first Conservative leader to be elected by his party to that position (previous leaders had 'emerged' after consultation among party grandees), succeeded as Prime Minister in the 1970 general election. His principal policy achievement was to negotiate Britain's entry into the EEC, after the principal obstacle to Britain's entry, the French President Charles de Gaulle, had resigned in 1969. Heath also brought us a U-turn in macroeconomic and industrial policy, and introduced anti-trade union legislation, which, alongside the first OPEC oil crisis, precipitated a coal miners' strike which led to the so-called three-day week in the winter of 1973–4. He lost the general election he called in February 1974, though only just; despite his party having fewer seats in the House of Commons than Labour, it had more of the popular vote. After Heath's failed attempt at forming a coalition with the Liberals, Labour took office.

1974–6 Harold Wilson (Labour)

Harold Wilson was once again Prime Minister, and promptly held a second general election in October 1974, where he gained a working majority in the House of Commons. After two years he claimed that he had 'gone around this track too many times', a reference to the recurring problems of government, and he resigned in 1976. Various conspiracy theories accompanied his resignation, as it was rare for a Prime Minister to give up power voluntarily; but as the longest-serving Labour Prime Minister to that date it seems that he was both tired of doing the job and becoming aware of the onset of Alzheimer's disease.

1976–9 James Callaghan (Labour)

Harold Wilson was replaced by an older man, the Foreign Secretary, James Callaghan, who became Prime Minister in 1976. He was immediately plunged into the teeth of the global stagflationary crisis of the late 1970s, involving high inflation and high unemployment, which had been brought about by the second OPEC oil crisis. He did some heretical thinking about Keynesian demand management, exclaiming that we could no longer spend our way out of recession, but failed to make the paradigm shift to monetarism. He upgraded the Polaris nuclear deterrent with the Chevaline programme. An old trade union man, he failed to recognise the threat to his government that the unions, prompted by the growing economic crisis, would present. He delayed the general election from the autumn of 1978 to the spring of 1979, during which time the so-called winter of discontent occurred, when there was widespread strike action, with even the dead being left unburied. He lost the election.

1979–90 Margaret Thatcher (Conservative)

The first woman Prime Minister, the first woman leader of the Conservative Party (elected party leader in 1975), and the longest continuously serving British Prime Minister of the modern era, Margaret Thatcher took power in 1979. The post-war consensus ended with her. She intended to use the free market to reverse the relative economic decline of the British economy, although she never achieved her goal of a minimalist state. She made the paradigm shift to monetarism in macroeconomic policy, privatised state-owned British industries and introduced quasi-market reforms into the state health and education services. However, some pragmatism was apparent as these services were not privatised. She replaced the American-developed Polaris nuclear deterrent with the newest American system, Trident; she won the Falklands War in 1982, and she strongly supported President George Bush in the first Gulf War. She won the 1983 and 1987 general elections to serve a record eleven and a half years as Prime Minister. Hubris was her eventual downfall when her party became fed up with her hectoring style and concluded that she had become an electoral liability. Her party dumped her in the autumn of 1990 and replaced her with the conciliatory John Major.

1990–7 John Major (Conservative)

John Major had no vision or ideology; his party misinterpreted these qualities as an ability to avoid alienating any part of his party, but in fact his lack of judgement enabled him to alienate just about every part of the party. He managed to win the 1992 general election by promulgating fears that a Labour government would raise taxes substantially. Major, when re-elected, then raised taxes substantially himself, presided over the ejection of sterling from the European Monetary System and failed to heal his party's rift over the issue of further political integration into the European Union, particularly concerning the Maastricht treaty. He was consequently punished with a landslide defeat in the 1997 general election.

1997 to date Tony Blair (Labour)

Tony Blair became Prime Minister at the age of forty-three in the 1997 general election without any previous experience in government, and would subsequently become the longest-serving Labour Prime Minister to date, winning the 2001 and 2005 general elections. He recognised that the strong ideologically driven style of Margaret Thatcher was preferable to the vagueness of John Major. In eighteen years of opposition the Labour Party had been transformed from a socialist party into one adopting the major policies of the Conservatives, including (for a while) their spending plans. This was necessary as the electorate had moved to the right. Privatisation was largely retained, low direct taxes were kept, as were quasi-market-based reforms to public services. However, government regulation of the economy grew exponentially and indirect taxation grew massively too, as did expenditure on the public services. In this regard there has been a gradual creep back towards traditional Labour Party policies.

2

The system of national governance

Introduction

The United Kingdom of Great Britain and Northern Ireland is ultimately governed from Westminster in London. The Channel Islands, notably Jersey and Guernsey, and the Isle of Man have separate systems of domestic governance, with the UK government exercising defence and foreign policy. Northern Ireland has enjoyed a similar status from time to time, interspersed with periods of direct rule from London. Scotland and Wales have had limited self-governance from the late 1990s. (Regional government is discussed in Chapter 3.)

The system of governance in Britain has changed only a little since 1945. It remains highly undemocratic: neither the Head of State nor the upper house of the legislature is democratically elected, and the lower house, although democratic, consistently produces governments elected by only a minority of the aggregate vote, a phenomenon explained below. This system of governance contrasts with the world's major industrial nations, particularly the republics: the USA, France, Germany, Italy, etc. Constitutional change in Britain has been limited to a gradual accretion of power to the executive at the expense of Parliament, though the government of Tony Blair has introduced the Freedom of Information Act and has also transformed the upper house from an hereditary chamber to one which is mostly appointed.

The system of governance in Britain can be described by examining the functions of the principal institutions of state. Britain does not have a written constitution, and therefore the system of governance and the functioning of these institutions is the result of a body of laws on the statute books (laws passed by Parliament) and 'accepted practices'. The latter refers to those practices where members of the governing elite have accrued powers to their offices, powers which have subsequently become accepted by the establishment. We identify and describe five discrete institutions of governance below.

Institutions of governance

The core executive

The core executive is the body which makes all the important political decisions. Unlike the other institutions set out below, the core executive is not well defined and will vary from government to government depending upon the objectives and character of the Prime Minister (PM). The PM is the most important member of the core executive and is based in the historic residence of 10 Downing Street in Westminster. In addition to the PM, the core executive usually comprises the other great officers of state, viz the Chancellor of the Exchequer, the Foreign Secretary, and one could also include the Home Secretary. The Chancellor of the Exchequer is the second most important after the PM as he or she is responsible for the economy. He or she is based at 11 Downing Street, with a connecting door to No. 10. The PM will generally appoint to those principal offices members of the governing party who are his or her closest associates, or occasionally those who have such support in the party that the PM feels obliged to appoint them to high office.

The office of Deputy Prime Minister has not been a constitutionally recognised post and so some governments have had one and others not. It is usually occupied by someone who the PM believes has some significant support within the party, but is not necessarily a close confidant of the PM. Thus the Deputy PM may not be part of the core executive. The core executive therefore usually comprises, inter alia, only *part* of the Cabinet.

The Cabinet, appointed by the PM from the governing party, comprises for the most part the heads of the various departments of government (most of whom are referred to as Secretaries of State). The Cabinet is generally appointed from members of Parliament (MPs) in the House of Commons, but occasionally from members of the House of Lords. The PM and the rest of the Cabinet (numbering twenty-seven in 2006) constitute the *official* executive body, but as we will see, it is not the Cabinet where the real power lies.

Like all politicians Cabinet members are 'generalists', in other words they do not necessarily have any specific specialised background relevant to the department of which they are in charge. To help them they have junior ministers, who are also drawn from the governing party in Parliament and appointed by the PM. To the less important Cabinet and junior ministerial positions the PM will often appoint young protégés or members of the party who do not share the PM's views but who represent significant factional interests in the party. The fact that all of these government officials are appointed by the Prime Minister gives the PM the power of 'patronage'.

This provides the PM with considerable authority vis-à-vis the Cabinet. The ability to hire and fire Cabinet and junior ministers enables the PM to exercise his or her own political influence over the ideology and detailed policy of the government. This means that aspirational politicians have a vested interest in supporting the PM. The PM is only constrained in his or her ability to fire, or fail to hire, members of the governing party when those politicians have considerable support in that party.

The principal opposition parties form shadow Cabinets, which are composed in the same way as the governing Cabinet but naturally lack executive authority. The leaders of opposition parties enjoy the same degree of patronage over shadow Cabinet members as does the PM over the Cabinet.

The government has an electoral advantage over the opposition parties because the PM can at his or her own behest ask the monarch to dissolve Parliament (call a general election) at any time within the maximum five-year term permitted. This means that a government will call a general election at a moment which is electorally propitious for itself.

The PM sets the agenda at Cabinet meetings, which enables him or her to determine the policy issues that he or she wants discussed. The PM sums up at the end of the meetings, which enables him or her to interpret the Cabinet discussion in a way favourable to the PM. The PM also determines the minutes of the meeting with the Cabinet Secretary (a civil servant). The minutes are not a verbatim record taken by a stenographer, but are notes which the PM can interpret, enabling the PM to give his or her own spin on Cabinet meeting discussions as they are finally recorded. There is also the notion of 'collective Cabinet responsibility', whereby, once a decision has been made in Cabinet, all Cabinet members are obliged to support it irrespective of their personal views on the matter. All of these functions provide the PM with a degree of authority over Cabinet which means that the modern PM has become more than *primus inter pares* (first among equals), the Victorian ideal for a PM.

Outside organisations constantly lobby members of the core executive as well as the principal opposition parties in order to influence policy decisions. The major corporations which finance the parties, and the major news organisations, enjoy a great deal of policy influence over the core executive. Governments will court major media proprietors and respond to policy concerns enunciated by the media.

Each head of department has a body of specialist civil servants advising them in their respective departments. This is something which the PM does not have as there is no Prime Ministerial Department, although there is a small

Cabinet Office. This means that the PM is relatively weak with respect to his or her Cabinet colleagues. Also, civil servants offer an inertia to policy change by dint of their degree of expertise through being permanent members of the system of governance, so maintaining a certain continuity in policy as governments change.

In order to provide the PM with independent expertise on policy matters to rectify these problems, Prime Ministers began to introduce special or private advisors. This process was accelerated by the government of Harold Wilson in 1974, but was taken much further by Margaret Thatcher. To this end she strengthened the 10 Downing Street Policy Unit and the PM's private office at the direct expense of the Cabinet Office. The Policy Unit is a particularly important part of the core executive for the following reasons: it acts as a think tank, provides policy advice direct to the PM on departmental issues, monitors the progress of departmental policies, deals with issues not dealt with by departments, alerts the PM to important policy issues and provides 'blue sky' policy development. This has changed the balance of power between the PM and the rest of the Cabinet as well as the balance between the PM and the civil service. As a consequence heads of departments acquired their own special advisors to strengthen their position vis-à-vis civil servants in their departments.

Special advisors are drawn from universities, industry, the City, the media and specialist research organisations. They enable politicians to exercise influence over the civil service in a way in which the politicians cannot on their own, given their generalist skills. Under Tony Blair's government the number of special advisors to the PM has grown yet further, as has the number working directly for Cabinet ministers. Also, the Blair government has given some of these special advisors the power to instruct civil servants, further reducing the influence of the civil service.

Policy presentation and news management have increasingly become fundamental to the core executive; thus the PM's press secretary has taken on heightened importance. The press secretary is not simply there to spin policy, but, being sensitive to prominent public issues, he or she has the power to influence the nature and content of policy.

To sum up, the core executive is therefore usually comprised of the PM and a sub-set of the Cabinet, plus a number of special advisors and the PM's press secretary.

The civil service

This is a permanent bureaucracy which exists under all governments. It comprises specialists in their respective fields (economics, health, transport, etc.) with permanent secretaries (officially titled permanent under-secretaries of state), who are the principal civil servants in each government department, including the Cabinet Office. The civil servants are ostensibly 'mere functionaries' carrying out the political will of the politicians in government. Many of the most important parts of the civil service are located in and around Whitehall in London. By the end of the Second World War there were 1.1 million civil servants; this number had fallen to 732,000 in 1979, and fell further to just over half a million by 1997. However, since then employment in the public sector has grown, standing at 563,000 at the end of 2005.

The civil service is very exclusive, comprising a disproportionate number of Oxford and Cambridge graduates from public schools. There is evidence that many civil servants were not educated and trained in skills pertinent to their work while at university. In 1966 Harold Wilson, when Labour PM, instituted a committee chaired by John Fulton to investigate these issues and make recommendations for reform. Fulton recommended among other things that civil servants should be recruited primarily on the basis of having specialist qualifications pertinent to their work, that recruitment should be broadened beyond the Oxbridge/public school sector, and that specialist management training should be provided. However, as the civil service itself took control of the implementation of these recommendations, it prevented fundamental reform. Of the recommendations only a Civil Service College for manage-ment training was introduced, and even then few civil servants were trained in it.

While Margaret Thatcher was PM, she was advised by Robin Ibbs on efficiency improvements in the civil service. He argued that though senior civil servants were effective at policy development, they had little aptitude for policy implementation. His report thus recommended that executive agencies should be created to perform the latter function. He also recommended that these agencies should enjoy a high degree of autonomy and be run by chief executives from outside the civil service. The Thatcher government accepted the Ibbs report and implemented its findings.

The civil service has, potentially, a significant impact on policy for a number of reasons: the civil servants tend to be better educated and qualified than the politicians for whom they work; the civil servants may spend much or all of their career in a particular department, unlike the politicians, who on average spend no more than two years in a post; and thus, despite their lack of specialist education, the civil servants acquire a high degree of expertise in their respective fields. These facts mean that the civil servants are often better qualified than the politicians to decide which policies will work best. Also the Cabinet Office is responsible for coordinating Cabinet committees of civil servants, which can be set up to address any policy issue and are usually headed by a senior politician, often the PM. These committees are shadowed by official committees, which are comprised of civil servants only. The civil service is further responsible for filtering or controlling the flow of work to government ministers, ostensibly to ensure that ministers do not have an excessive workload. However, this confers considerable powers on the civil service as it enables them to exercise control over the information which ministers receive.

The civil service forms communities with vested interest groups; examples of this are the Department for Work and Pensions with the Trades Union Congress (TUC) and the Department of Trade and Industry with the Confederation of British Industry (CBI). In consequence these communities can be highly influential in policy formation.

If the core executive lacks drive and clear direction, then instead of policy being decided in Cabinet and the politicians instructing the civil servants as to which policies to carry out, it is the civil servants who tell the politicians which policies will work best, and the politicians then explain these policies in Cabinet – precisely the opposite of what is supposed to happen! The civil servants have a vested interest in this version of events, because if no new policies are introduced the workload of the civil service does not increase. This does much to explain the elements of continuity in government policy between Labour and Conservative ministries since the Second World War. It is precisely this inertia in policy created by the civil service which the intro-duction of special advisors was intended to overcome. A driven government with a clear agenda and special advisors to argue the intellectual case will overcome the inertia.

The accountability of the civil service is a vital constitutional issue. It is argued that civil servants are accountable to elected politicians and thus to the electorate. The creation of executive agencies with a high degree of autonomy does, however, question this line of accountability. But, as we have seen, the civil service has been responsible for a great deal of influence in policy development since 1945, and whereas the government can be replaced by the electorate, the civil service cannot.

The monarchy

The monarch is Head of State, and the PM is head of the monarch's government. The monarch is hereditary. The eldest (surviving) son of the monarch always succeeds to the throne; only if there is no son does the eldest daughter succeed. A succeeding son becomes King, and his wife normally Queen. A succeeding daughter becomes Queen, but her husband does not become King, merely Prince. The current line of succession can trace its roots to the Hanoverians, the first of whom, George I, succeeded to the throne in 1714. The royal family's surname was Saxe-Coburg und Gotha until late in the First World War, when it was changed to Windsor. There have been just two monarchs since 1945, King George VI until his death from lung cancer in 1952, and his eldest daughter, Queen Elizabeth II, since then. George VI was under the impression that constitutionally he could intervene in the system of governance in a time of crisis, although he did not so do during the most important time of crisis in British history, the Second World War. Elizabeth II is under no such illusion. This is known as a 'constitutional monarchy': officially one which is bound by constitutional arrangements determined in Parliament, really one which lacks any executive authority.

The monarch's powers appear not inconsiderable at first blush: he or she gives the seals of office to the PM (appoints the PM); has the power to dissolve Parliament, in other words call a general election (the House of Commons only as the Lords is unelected); delivers the speech at the opening of each session of Parliament setting out the government's legislative programme (the Queen's Speech); and gives Royal Assent to laws passed by Parliament (only with the monarch's signature do they become law). The monarch is also head of the armed forces and head of the Church of England (the established Protestant Christian church). The 'royal prerogative' gives the monarch the power to declare war and the authority to sign international treaties.

In reality, however, the monarch can only appoint as Prime Minister the leader of the party with a majority in the House of Commons; he or she can only dissolve Parliament (within the maximum five years permitted) if the PM asks him or her so to do; the speech the Monarch gives in Parliament is written by the government; and Royal Assent to laws is given automatically by the monarch when those laws have passed through Parliament. The PM, not the monarch, appoints the bishops in the Church of England; originally the PM had wide discretion in this regard, but Margaret Thatcher changed this so the Church now provides a list of two for each appointment from which the PM chooses. It is also the PM, not the monarch, who has ultimate responsibility for using the armed forces and determining the international treaties to which Britain is signatory.

If there is a 'hung' Parliament, that is, there is no party with an overall majority, then the monarch will ask the leader of the largest party either to form a minority government or to form a coalition with one or more other parties, depending on the leader's choice. If the leader believes he or she cannot do this, then fresh elections will be called.

Thus the monarch has no executive powers, but only a ceremonial role.

Parliament

Parliament is the legislature and is comprised of two chambers: the House of Commons and the House of Lords. It is located in Westminster.

The House of Commons (historically this means 'communes' rather than 'commoners') is the democratic chamber and is comprised of salaried members of Parliament (MPs). The country is divided into 646 constituencies and the electorate resident in each constituency votes for a candidate to represent their interests in the House of Commons. The Commons is therefore a representative chamber where members ostensibly employ their own judgement in parliamentary debates, not a chamber of delegates who are obliged to carry out the wishes of their voters or of their party. However, as we shall see, the party leadership exercises considerable discipline over them.

The constituency boundaries are intended to ensure that a roughly equal number of the electorate is resident in each of them, so some, such as those in the sparsely populated areas of Scotland, are geographically much larger than those in the densely populated areas of the south-east of England. The Boundary Commission periodically adjusts the constituency boundaries as demographic movement over time changes the population in each constituency.

Ministers aside, the House of Commons has three particularly prominent offices. There is the Speaker, who is an elected MP but is required to disavow party affiliation and thus remain politically neutral in debates. He or she calls members to speak and has powers to call the House to order. The Speaker has three deputies, who each remain affiliated to their party. Then there is the Leader of the House, an MP of the governing party, who is appointed by the PM and is responsible for managing government legislative business in the Commons. Finally there is the Father of the House, who is the MP who has served the longest in the House.

When the House of Commons is dissolved at the behest of the PM within the maximum five-year term, all members of the Commons are obliged to stand for re-election in a general election (except, of course, the retiring MPs, who are replaced by their parties with fresh candidates). If an individual member retires, resigns or dies in office during a parliament then a by-election is called, where an election takes place in the vacant constituency alone. The main parties field candidates in every Commons constituency, while small parties field candidates in some constituencies, and there are some candidates who stand as independents. The major parties have local parties for each of the constituencies and these are responsible for selecting candidates, usually at interview from a shortlist. They or their party are required to provide a financial deposit of £500, which is returned if their vote exceeds a 5 per cent threshold and not returned otherwise. This is to deter frivolous candidates, though it tends to deter just *poor* frivolous candidates!

MPs are elected on a 'first-past-the-post' system; in other words, the candidate in each constituency with more votes than any other candidate wins. This means that because at least three parties contest each constituency, in many cases the sum of the votes cast for all of the candidates who do not win will exceed the votes cast for the winning candidate (the winning candidate has only a minority of the total votes cast). As governments are formed by the party with a majority of members in the Commons, this means that invariably the governing party will have received only a minority of the 'popular vote', the aggregate votes cast in the general election. This is entirely a consequence of the first-past-the-post electoral system combined with an electoral contest that involves more than two parties. With only two parties, or an electoral system based on proportional representation, this problem would not occur.

The House of Lords is composed of the Lords Spiritual, that is, the senior bishops, and the Lords Temporal, the lay members. The latter include the Law Lords, who are the senior judges. There were a total of 666 members of the House of Lords in 2004. None of them are democratically elected.

The role of Speaker of the Lords was undertaken by the Lord Chancellor for centuries, who was also a Cabinet minister and head of the judiciary in England and Wales. Unlike the Speaker of the Commons, the Speaker of the Lords cannot call members to speak or call the House to order. He sits on a seat known as the woolsack. Like the Commons, the Lords has a Leader of the House, who is a member of the governing party and is appointed by the PM. It is the Leader, and not the Speaker, who is responsible for procedural matters in the Lords. These offices, together with all members of the Lords who are appointed by the PM as government ministers, plus the Law Lords, all receive a salary; all other peers are unpaid, but do receive expenses. The Gentleman Usher of the Black Rod is a ceremonial functionary in the Lords and is also responsible for security.

Because the Lords is undemocratic, the 1911 Parliament Act was introduced to end the ability of the Lords to veto a law passed by the Commons, but it allowed the Lords to delay one by a maximum of two years, with the exception of a law intended to extend the duration of a Parliament. The Act also reduced the maximum duration between general elections from seven years to its current five years. The 1949 Parliament Act reduced the Lords' ability to delay a law to one year.

The Lords was a chamber comprised exclusively of hereditary aristocrats or peers until 1958. This gave the Conservative Party a political advantage because most of these peers were Conservative Party supporters. From 1958 life peers were introduced, who as their name implies were not hereditary. This was a way by which the major parties could introduce specialists into Parliament without their being elected. Parties would bestow life peerages upon those who were affiliated to a party and had some body of knowledge to contribute in legislative debate or who were to act as government ministers or who had simply provided finance to a party.

The Blair government has taken this evolution of the Lords one step further through the 1999 House of Lords Act, which abolished the right of all but ninety-two hereditary peers to vote in the Lords. Thus the House of Lords has become essentially an appointed-only chamber. Proposals have been put forward by a government-sponsored commission to democratise the Lords in some form but none has been enacted as yet. The major parties have no vested interest in democratising the Lords, as they can pack it with their own appointees.

Both the Commons and the Lords are responsible for debating and legislating (making laws). Prime Minister's Question Time, which occurs weekly in the Commons, is where opposition parties and ordinary MPs have the facility to question the PM. Although the Commons is the lower chamber and the Lords the upper chamber, it is the Commons which has primacy as only it is elected. Bills (policy proposals) can be introduced in either chamber, except for those concerning the vital issue of fiscal policy, which have to be introduced in the Commons and which the Lords is required to pass without amendment. The Lords is further constrained by the Salisbury convention: once elected to office, a party's manifesto policy commitments when put into a Bill cannot be voted down by the Lords at second reading.

Bills must have three readings in each chamber before they become law (Acts); after each reading they are usually voted on. The governing party is responsible for bringing most of the Bills before Parliament, though some legislation (private members' Bills) is initiated by individual MPs of any party, rather than by the government. Assent by both chambers (with the provisos of the 1911 and 1949 Parliament Acts) is required before a Bill can become law, though either chamber can amend Bills, and these amendments require assent by both Houses. The Lords spends two-thirds of its time amending bills; thus it is primarily a revising chamber.

Of those MPs who are not government ministers, the backbench MPs, some will serve on House of Commons select committees, which scrutinise the policies of each government department. Each committee comprises MPs from all the major political parties. These committees have the power to summon both civil servants and government ministers to be questioned; they also take evidence from experts outside Parliament, and they write reports. There are also House of Lords select committees and joint committees, which draw members from both Houses.

A Parliamentary legislative session runs for one year, starting and ending in the autumn. The State Opening of Parliament is a ceremony where all Commons and Lords members congregate in the Lords chamber. The monarch is present and he or she reads the Queen's (or King's) Speech, which informs them of the government's legislative programme for the new parliamentary session. Terminating a parliamentary session is referred to as 'proroguing' Parliament. Parliament does not sit at weekends or on public holidays; it has a half-term break in February and 'recesses' (holidays) at Easter, at the end of May, in the summer and at Christmas. Most of the Houses' work is conducted in the afternoons and evenings.

According to Britain's unwritten constitution, parliament is sovereign, that is, it is the ultimate law-making body in the land. This means that only by a majority vote of politicians in Parliament can any law be enacted. In reality, the leadership of each party can coerce its politicians in Parliament to vote in the way the leadership wants through the 'whipping' system.

The whips are politicians of each party in both the Commons and the Lords, under the authority of each party's Chief Whip, who are instructed by the party leadership to discover the voting intentions of their party's politicians in Parliament. If these politicians wish to vote against the leadership, then the whips will point out that as the leader has the power of patronage, these politicians will not advance their careers into government (or the shadow

Cabinet) if they oppose the leader. Recalcitrant politicians may 'lose the whip', that is, no longer be considered members of the party, at least for some specified period. In extreme cases MPs can be deselected as candidates in their constituencies, meaning that they will not be their party's candidate in future elections. Thus the leadership exercise a high degree of control over their party in Parliament.

Also, since Britain joined the European Economic Community (now the European Union) in January 1973, all legislation of the Westminster Parliament has been subordinate to EU law. As we will see in the addendum to Chapter 14, it is the core executives of the member states who ultimately determine EU law.

The judiciary

The Law Lords (in the House of Lords) act as the ultimate court of appeal in the United Kingdom for civil law cases, and for cases of criminal law in England, Wales and Northern Ireland but not Scotland, which has its own legal system.

The Blair government has abolished the office of the Lord Chancellor and has introduced the Department for Constitutional Affairs with a secretary of state, which has taken over the responsibilities of the Lord Chancellor's Department. The government has also proposed the introduction of a 'Supreme Court' to replace the Law Lords, and a new Lords Speaker who is not a government minister.

Law Lords, when asked to adjudicate on matters of law, may interpret the written law in a way rather different to that intended by the politicians who framed it. This means that if a government department introduces a policy which prima facie violates a law on the statute books, it can be a matter of interpretation by the judge as to whether the department is found to be acting ultra vires (in other words, beyond their legal authority). If they are so found then the department is obliged to change its policy so as to be consistent with the judge's interpretation of the law. However, the government can if it wishes, introduce retrospective legislation through Parliament to make legal those very actions which a department had earlier taken, and which had been found to be illegal.

All other members of the judiciary – all other judges, barristers, solicitors and the courts – exist to implement the laws made by Parliament.

Conclusion

It is a mistake to suggest that, simply because the electorate are faced with alternative parties at a general election, this by itself constitutes a democratic system. As we have seen, it is becuase we have a first-past-the-post electoral system and yet more than two parties contesting elections that the system is undemocratic.

However, the reduction in the influence of the civil service over policy decisions, which was considerable in the first few decades after the Second World War, and the increased influence of the core executive (including special advisors from outside the civil service and Parliament) in determining policy decsisons, is a good advance. This is because it enables the core executive to enact its own policies by overcoming the inertia of the civil sevice; at a general election, if the electorate object to those policies then the core executive can be dispensed with, but there is no way of changing the permanent civil service.

To the extent that change occurs in the system of governance, it continues as it has always done, principally by small increments of evolution, not revolution.

3

Local and regional government

Introduction

There has been little devolution of power from central government to the local level; in fact, if anything there has been movement the other way. Local government thus has few powers and is reliant upon central government for the bulk of its finances, and because of this central government exercises considerable power over it. The only significant exception is London, which now has an executive mayor for the first time.

In the years following the Second World War England and Wales had a single-tier system of local government in seventy-nine county boroughs, plus a two-tier system of forty-eight counties in which there were a total of 415 rural districts, 491 urban districts and 285 municipal boroughs. Scotland had a very complex system of some 400 local government bodies: counties, also counties of cities, plus burghs and districts. London was governed by the London County Council (LCC), under which there were twenty-eight metropolitan boroughs plus the City of London authority.

This system was altered first with the 1963 Local Government Act, but then quite significantly by the Local Government Act of 1972 for England and Wales (enacted in 1974) and the 1973 Act for Scotland (enacted in 1975). In England and Wales this established a two-tier system of counties and district authorities. Some counties were abolished and merged to create a new total of thirty-nine non-metropolitan or 'shire' counties, under which there were 296 districts in all. The major cities outside London were transformed into six new 'metropolitan counties' containing thirty-six metropolitan districts. In London, the LCC had already been replaced (in 1965) by the larger Greater London Council (GLC), under which there were thirty-two boroughs and the City of London authority. In Scotland the very complex system was simplified into nine regional authorities, under which were established fifty-three district authorities.

The function of the counties in local government was to undertake strategic planning and provide police, fire and school services plus refuse disposal; whereas the districts were responsible for building regulations, housing policy, environmental health issues and refuse collection. There remained some local parish authorities within the counties as well.

The Conservative government of Margaret Thatcher wished to reduce the influence of largely Labour-controlled city councils and so the Local Government Act of 1985 (enacted 1986) retained the thirty-nine English and Welsh shire counties and their districts, but it abolished the metropolitan counties and left a single tier of the thirty-six metropolitan districts. The Act also abolished the GLC, leaving a single tier of the thirty-two boroughs and the City of London authority. The powers of the GLC and the metropolitan counties were transferred to the boroughs and to specially created joint boards. In 1999, the New Labour government of Tony Blair reintroduced an upper tier of local government for London in the guise of the Greater London Authority (GLA) in addition to the second tier of boroughs, but with greatly reduced powers compared to the GLC.

Meanwhile, a number of unitary authorities were created between 1995 and 1998. Like the metropolitan boroughs, these are single-tier administrations which have responsibility for every aspect of local government. In 2006 there were forty-six such authorities in England, plus thirty-four shire counties divided into 239 districts. Since 2006 local government has been administered by the Department for Communities and Local Government.

Local government

Local government employs two million people (in 2006) and accounts for approximately a quarter of total public expenditure. Since 1945 the responsibilities of local authorities have expanded to include the provision of a wide range of welfare, health and recreational services and planning functions. However, the Thatcher government's reforms of the National Health Service (Chapter 7) and state education provision (Chapter 8) and its privatisation programme (Chapter 11) were to result in the removal from local authority responsibility of health service functions and some educational service functions and the transference of school meal provision and refuse collection to private contractors, albeit financed from the state. Also, the utilities of gas, electricity and water, which had originally been partly municipally owned and were subsequently put under the control of regional boards, were privatised by the Thatcher government (Chapter 11).

Legally, central government supervenes over local government; this means that central government prescribes their areas of activity through parliamentary legislation, activities which local government is either required to carry out, or permitted to do so on a discretionary basis. Not only is this control of local government by central government exercised legally, but, as local government raises only a small proportion of its finances through the local tax system, it is reliant upon central government for the bulk of its finances. Central government supervises local authority administration of the police, the fire brigade and schools with an inspection system. Local authorities require central government consent for introducing by-laws, important building plans and the appointment of key local officials.

Local authorities are composed of elected councillors who have executive powers and a permanent civil service of functionaries to carry out policy. There are usually between sixty and 100 councillors in county councils, and between fifty and eighty in districts and boroughs. Councillors are mostly drawn from the political parties which contest parliamentary elections, though some are independent; this means that councils will often be run by a majority of councillors from one of the major parties, although if no such party has a majority the council is described as being under 'no overall control'. Candidates standing for local election are not required to submit a deposit, which candidates for the Westminster Parliament must do, but local authority candidates' election expenses are limited. Councillors are not paid a salary, but instead receive a loss of earnings allowance.

The counties are subdivided for electoral purposes into divisions, each of which returns a single councillor in elections; this also applies to all councillors of every local body in Scotland. The districts and boroughs are divided into wards, each of which returns three councillors in elections. County councillors, those councillors representing London boroughs and all councillors in Scotland are subject to elections every four years. In the districts, two-thirds of the councillors are also subject to elections every four years. The remaining third, along with all of the councillors representing districts in metropolitan areas (that is, cities outside London), are divided into three groups, each of which is subject to elections in each of the intervening three years within the four-year electoral cycle. Although this is a more democratic system than is used for central government, it has the disadvantage that policy decisions are continually frustrated by the annual change in the structure of the ruling party's councillors. Also, it obviously results in additional election expenses. The chairman of each council and the mayor of each borough are drawn from the elected councillors and are subject to annual elections by the other councillors. Aldermen used to be elected in the same manner as chairmen and mayors, and served a six-year term. However, this office was abolished in 1974 as aldermen added little to the effective functioning of authorities but were less democratic: being drawn from among the councillors, they tended to be self-perpetuating and had a longer term in office.

The civil service for local administration, the paid employees who carry out policy, consists of the chief executive (previously known as the clerk of the council), the council administrators, plus all of the employees of the organisations under the council's control, such as school teachers (those still subject to local authority control), transport staff and other directly employed staff. Local authority employees are appointed and dismissed by the elected council, and are expected to be politically impartial.

Councils are given considerable internal discretion as to how they conduct their affairs, but all councils must meet at least four times a year, and the public and press are admitted to observe, though councils may meet in closed sessions if deemed necessary. The council chairman is usually neutral but has a casting vote. Councils have a system of committees, each of which deals with a principal area of policy and puts forward policy proposals to be considered by the council. The council may accept or reject these proposals or return them to the appropriate committee for further policy development. There is a principal committee on most councils, referred to as the Policy and Resources Committee, which is comprised of the council chairman and senior council members of the majority party. It acts in the way the central government Cabinet functions in giving overall direction to council work.

About a third of total council revenue is raised through local taxes; until 1988 this was raised via a tax system known as rates. This was a property-based local tax the value of which was determined by the nominal annual rentable value of the property, and which the owner was required to pay. Councils also borrow to undertake capital investments; they do this through the banks, the Stock Exchange and from central government. However, loans are subject to the consent of central government. The rest of local government finance is provided by a central government grant. The 1958 Local Government Act scrapped the system whereby grants were provided for specific issues (health, education, etc.) and introduced a general grant system which gave councils considerable discretion in how it was spent. The 1966 Local Government Act increased the proportion of central government grant provision relative to local tax by 1 per cent per annum. The Thatcher government, however, reversed this and reduced government grant provision; it also sought to control that portion of local authorities' expenditure financed from local taxes in order to try and achieve its aim of reducing total government expenditure. It did this through the Local Government Act of 1982, which required government approval before authorities could levy a supplementary rate to address unforeseen expenditure, and the 1984 Local Government Act, which provided the government with wide-ranging powers to cap rates, and which effectively took away the executive authority of Councils over the value of rates levied.

However, the government decided that more fundamental reform was necessary to curb high-spending Labour-controlled local authorities and decided to change the local tax system to accomplish this. This desire was fuelled by the fact that during the Thatcher periods of government, as often occurs, the electorate were employing local authority elections as referenda on central government performance, and when these elections occurred mid-term between general elections, they consistently reflected opposition to the government. Given the long period of continuous Conservative government, this meant that ever more local authorities were coming under Labour control.

The existing system of rates meant that a large proportion of the population, viz. those who were not property owners, were receiving local services without having to pay for them. This group had a vested interest in demanding more local services, and as they constituted a large proportion of the electorate, local authorities found it necessary to offer ever more services. Margaret Thatcher wanted to make local authorities more accountable to their electorate and to make the electorate take account of the expense of policies when they voted. To this end a new local tax was introduced which was a flat-rate charge upon all adults in return for local authority services. Introduced in 1988, it was officially called the community charge but it became known colloquially as the 'poll tax'.

However, the tax was difficult to collect, as many evaded it by moving frequently. Also its value proved to be double the initial estimates. This was because the tax had been devised without the Chancellor of the Exchequer, Nigel Lawson, being involved; he opposed it and would not provide additional subsidy to reduce its value. It was suggested that the old 'rates' system and the new tax should run together for an introductory period (known as dual running), but this was finally rejected. The tax was first introduced in Scotland and protests resulted.

Thatcher assumed that high-spending local authorities would be blamed for imposing a high poll tax and would consequently lose votes, but it was in fact Thatcher who was blamed by the electorate and opinion polls showed a fall in support for the government as a result. Many Conservatives, such as Michael Heseltine, were keenly aware of this problem and he wrote an article to this effect, and because many middle-class families were worse off as a result of the tax there was a Conservative backbench rebellion. Thatcher's intransigence over this tax, and opposition from her own party, were factors in her replacement as party leader and Prime Minister by John Major. Major appointed Heseltine as Secretary of State for the Environment and charged him with replacing the tax. The community charge was replaced with the council tax in 1993, which, like the rates, is a property-based tax but is based on property sale value. A number of value bands exist, referred to by letters of the alphabet – the higher the band the higher the tax charged. It is thus a progressive system.

Local government for London

London had been governed by the London County Council (LCC) since 1889, under which there were twenty-eight metropolitan boroughs plus the City of London authority. However, on 1 April 1965 it was replaced by the Greater London Council (GLC). Geographically the GLC took responsibility for nearly all of Middlesex and some parts of other adjacent counties previously not covered by the LCC, and in consequence there were now thirty-two boroughs as well as the City of London authority. Both organisations were two-tier systems with the boroughs as the lower tier. Joint boards were established to govern transport, the fire brigade and civil defence.

In 1980 a left-wing Labour Party group under Ken Livingstone took control of the GLC. In 1985 the government of Margaret Thatcher chose to abolish the GLC in order to eliminate this high-spending Labour-controlled local government body. This left a single tier of the boroughs and the City of London authority.

The New Labour government of Tony Blair was impressed with the concept of executive mayors in American cities who could address deep-seated problems, and he wanted such a post for London. A referendum was conducted amongst the London electorate to ask for approval for the proposal. This approval was duly given, and the Greater London Authority Act of 1999 brought the Greater London Authority (GLA) and its elected mayor into existence. This restored an upper tier of governance for London.

The mayor of London is not to be confused with the unelected Lord Mayor of London, which is an ancient post. The Lord Mayor is head of the City of London authority, also known as the Corporation of London, and presides over its governing bodies: the Court of Aldermen and the Court of Common Council. The Lord Mayor is also the chief magistrate of the City of London, is admiral of the Port of London, and acts as business promoter to the financial centre of the City of London, both at home and abroad. The Lord Mayor functions quite separately from the mayor and the GLA.

The mayor of London is a directly elected and salaried position, with a personal staff of thirty. The GLA incorporates the London Assembly, which comprises twenty-five elected and salaried members. The GLA has a secretariat (administrative staff) of approximately 600, including a chief executive. The assembly appoints the permanent staff, and the deputy mayor is appointed from its ranks by the mayor. The mayor and the assembly are elected contemporaneously and both serve for a term of four years. Assembly members annually elect a chair and a deputy chair. The electoral system employed to elect the assembly members is intended to ensure that the outcome reflects the aggregate votes cast in London.

The GLA has responsibility for the following functions: policing, the fire brigade, planning, culture, environmental issues, health services and transport. The mayoral responsibilities cover the Metropolitan Police Authority, the London Fire and Emergency Planning Authority, the London Development Agency and Transport for London (regarding the latter, see Chapter 10).

The mayor must submit his or her budget to the assembly for approval, and is required to present all his or her principal policies to it, as well as consulting the assembly and attending at least ten assembly question time sessions annually. The assembly scrutinises the mayor's activities, can make policy proposals to the mayor and can amend the mayor's budget providing it has at least a two-thirds majority. The assembly provides members to serve on the Metropolitan Police Authority, the London Fire and Emergency Planning Authority and the London Development Agency. All reports and records of meetings are made public and the mayor and assembly are required to attend a public question-and-answer session twice a year.

The total GLA budget was £4.7 billion in 2002/3, of which the administration cost was approximately £49.9 million. Central government provides a grant for the vast majority of this budget with London council tax payers contributing only a small proportion.

Regional government in Scotland and Wales

There has been a revolution in regional government in Britain, with Scotland and Wales enjoying a parliament and an assembly respectively since the late 1990s, and Northern Ireland having its own parliament again after many years' absence.

Scotland and Wales have long had parties which field candidates only in the constituencies of these countries for representation in the Westminster Parliament: the Scottish Nationalist Party (SNP) and Plaid Cymru. But the three main parties of British national politics also field candidates, and these tend to receive more support than the SNP and Plaid Cymru. The major change in the politics of Scotland and Wales is devolution.

In the 1970s the Labour government proposed the notion of devolved governments for Scotland and Wales, and to this end referenda were held in 1979 to obtain the Scottish and Welsh electorate's approval. A simple majority was required for approval, but also a 40 per cent threshold was set for turnout. The majority was achieved in Scotland but not the turnout threshold; thus, despite the fact that work had largely been concluded on a Scottish Parliament building, the proposal was scrapped. In Wales voters decisively rejected the proposal. The Thatcher government came into power soon afterwards and had no interest in devolved government. It wasn't until the Labour government of Tony Blair that the proposal was revived for a Scottish Parliament in Edinburgh, having primary and secondary legislative powers over domestic matters, and a Welsh Assembly in Cardiff with reduced powers. Referenda were held in both countries, with a decisive majority achieved in Scotland and a slender one in Wales. The bodies came into existence in 1999.

Most of the Members of the Scottish Parliament (MSPs) and Welsh Assembly Members (AMs) are elected by the same first-past-the-post system as used in the Westminster Parliament. However, a small proportion of additional members are elected by proportional representation to ensure the composition of the bodies is genuinely representative of voting intentions, a feature notably absent at Westminster. The Scottish Parliament has 129 members of which seventy-three are directly elected, and has fifty-six additional members elected proportionally. The Welsh Assembly has sixty members of which forty are directly elected, with twenty additional ones elected proportionally.

The electoral process functions in the following way: each voter has two votes, one for their constuency member and one for the additional member. The constituency member is elected under the first-past-the-post system, but the additional member is elected by the voter putting a cross against a party, not a candidate. The number of votes for each party's additional members are not counted within the Westminster constituency boundaries but within the larger European Parliament constituencies (see Addendum), of which Scotland has eight and Wales five. In Scotland seven additional members are elected per European Parliament constituency and in Wales four. The number of seats each party has won in each European constituency under the first-past-the-post system, plus one, is then divided into the number of votes cast for each party in each European constituency. The party with the largest figure resulting from that calculation will win the first additional member. Now the process is repeated with the party having the additional member seat added to its total, and continues to be repeated until all additional seats are allocated.

In Scotland the executive comprises a Cabinet of eighteen members and a head of government known as the First Minister. The executive, together with two law officers, has taken over the functions of the Secretary of State for Scotland in the Westminster government, and administers a legal system which has since antiquity been different from that in England and Wales.

The Scottish Parliament has full legislative powers but only in the following fields, prescribed by the Westminster Parliament: economic development, local government, health, education, housing, trade, transport, environment, agriculture, food standards, forestry, fisheries, sport, the arts, criminal and civil law, courts, prisons, the police and fire services. But there are many powers which the Westminster Parliament has reserved for itself: constitutional matters concerning the United Kingdom, foreign policy, defence and national security, border controls, common markets for goods and services, employment law, social security, regulation of the professions, transport safety, nuclear safety, matters relating to abortion law, cinema licensing, monetary policy and fiscal policy, with the exception that the Scottish Parliament is able to raise or lower the basic marginal rate of income tax by up to three percentage points.

Scottish MPs sit in the Westminster Parliament in order to address those issues of importance to Scotland not covered by the Scottish Parliament. But they can also vote on issues relating to the rest of Britain which have no direct relevance to Scotland. This issue was highlighted in the so-called West Lothian question, a phrase coined by Tam Dalyell as MP for the former Scottish constituency of West Lothian. The question is whether it is fair that this anomaly should exist.

The Welsh Assembly is much weaker. It has an executive, comprising a Cabinet and a First Minister, but does not have the same legislative powers. The executive has taken responsibility for those areas which had previously been overseen by the Secretary of State for Wales in the Westminster government. These areas are health and social services, education, housing, industry and training, economic development, transport, agriculture and food, environment, local government, planning, arts and culture, sport and recreation, and heritage. The assembly also has the power to amend Westminster legislation in some cases.

The Blair government also had plans for a number of regional assemblies in England to perform similar functions to those of the Welsh Assembly. However, lack of interest amongst the electorate subsequently led to the abandonment of this proposal.

Regional government in Northern Ireland

The issue of home rule in Ireland (the independence of the island of Ireland) had been debated since the nineteenth century and had culminated in the decision of the Prime Minister, David Lloyd George, to partition Ireland in 1921, creating the 26-county independent Republic of Ireland or Eire, with its predominantly Catholic population and capital in Dublin. Eire had dominion status for the subsequent decade, and then complete independence after that. Partition also created the six-county province of Northern Ireland or Ulster (historically Ulster included three counties not in Northern Ireland) with its predominantly Protestant population who were hostile to home rule because it would mean domination by the Catholic majority in the island of Ireland. Thus Northern Ireland remained part of the United Kingdom. The intention of partition was to create a 'built-in' majority Protestant population for Northern Ireland, a fact which would cause constant friction with the Catholic minority in the province from then onwards.

Northern Ireland was self-governing with its own party system (British political parties do not operate there). The Parliament of Northern Ireland produced a government and a Prime Minister and consisted of two chambers, a directly elected House of Commons with fifty-two members, and a Senate of twenty-six members, who were elected by the Commons via proportional representation. It was located at Stormont, a suburb of Belfast, and had legislative powers with regard to all issues directly pertaining to Northern Ireland. The only major issues over which the Westminster Parliament had sovereignty were defence and some elements of taxation.

The majority Protestant population would elect parties to government which reflected their sectarian Protestant beliefs, the Ulster Unionist Party (UUP, often known as the Official Unionists) and later also the Democratic Unionist Party (DUP), who were loyal to the constitutional link with Britain. Thus Protestant groups became known as loyalists. The minority Catholic republican or nationalist community, who believed ultimately in the reunification of Ireland with rule from Dublin, would be represented by the Social Democratic and Labour Party (SDLP) and particularly by Sinn Fein, the political wing of the armed paramilitary group the Provisional Irish Republican Army (IRA). The IRA was 'provisional' on the basis that once the British had been expelled from Northern Ireland there would be a permanent force to defend a united Ireland. There is also the non-sectarian Alliance Party.

In 1969, the Home Secretary, James Callaghan, authorised the deployment of British troops into Northern Ireland to address the republican paramilitary armed threat, principally from the IRA. Sustained IRA activity, and counter-terrorist activity by paramilitary groups loyal to the constitutional link with Britain, would necessitate a permanent British military presence in the province.

In 1972, the Northern Ireland government collapsed due to the deteriorating security situation and direct rule from Westminster was introduced under a newly created Northern Ireland Office (NIO). The NIO was a government department with a secretary of state in charge; it was given responsibility for constitutional and security matters, viz. policing and criminal justice. Parliamentary representation was now to be in Westminster with Northern Ireland divided into eighteen constituences and the Northern Ireland parties fielding candidates.

Edward Heath's government attempted to reintroduce the Northern Ireland Parliament and government with a power-sharing agreement between the loyalist and nationalist politicians, known as the Sunningdale agreement. However, relations between the parties quickly broke down and so Sunningdale subsequently failed, and direct rule from Westminster continued until the late 1990s.

In 1985 Margaret Thatcher was persuaded by the Prime Minister of the Republic of Ireland, Garret FitzGerald, to sign the Anglo-Irish agreement, which gave the Republic a say in Northern Ireland's politics. This was intended to quell the violence by marginalising Sinn Fein and the IRA and so enabling a return to democratic politics. The agreement was a curious anomaly for Thatcher, as it meant that a foreign power had direct influence in domestic UK governance, something which she was ideologically opposed to and accepted only out of pragmatism.

In 1993 Sinn Fein and the IRA signalled that they were prepared to begin a process of de-escalating the violence and moving to a power-sharing agreement. They did this because census information had indicated that the indigenous Catholic population of Northern Ireland was growing relative to the Protestant population, and thus republicans would be increasingly able to influence political decisions in a democratic framework. This caused a reversal in British government policy: instead of marginalising Sinn Fein and the IRA, they sought to make them central to the democratic political system. This culminated in the Downing Street declaration in December 1993, which constituted a public enunciation of this policy change. As a direct consequence the IRA announced a cessation of terrorist acts in August the following year and the loyalist paramilitary groups did similarly in October.

In 1995 the British and Irish governments agreed a document called 'Frameworks for the Future'. This posited the idea of a North–South institutional body to strengthen the 1985 Anglo-Irish agreement of cross-border cooperation between Northern Ireland and the Republic, though it was fiercely opposed by loyalist politicians in the North. The issue of decommissioning terrorist weapons (removing them from use) was essential if progress towards non-violent democratic politics was to be accomplished, though achieving it would be fraught with difficulty. This decommissioning process was formerly codified in the Mitchell report in 1996. Consequently, elections to a new Northern Ireland forum were organised for May 1996, and all-party talks were initiated shortly thereafter. This culminated in the so-called Good Friday agreement to restore a devolved Northern Ireland Parliament and government.

The Good Friday or Belfast agreement of April 1998 was ratified by a referendum in May and by legislation, the Northern Ireland Act, in the same year. It brought into existence the Northern Ireland Assembly, with both legislative and executive authority for all matters relating to Northern Ireland, reserved matters (foreign affairs and defence) being retained by the

Westminster Parliament. The Belfast agreement also formally brought into existence the North–South Ministerial Council for cross-border cooperation. The agreement is complex so as to ensure thorough engagement by both Protestant and Catholic political groups and hence to quell violent discontent.

The Northern Ireland Assembly comprises 108 members, six from each of the eighteen constituencies which elect Westminster MPs. The executive is made up of the head of government, the First Minister, and the deputy First Minister, who lead the Cabinet, known as the Executive Committee of Ministers. As it was anticipated that the First Minister would be Protestant (the majority population) and the deputy Catholic, they are both elected conjointly, and they jointly specify the number of ministers in the executive responsible for the various Northern Ireland departments of government. This is to ensure that both religious communities are strongly represented in the executive. Those parties represented in the assembly select ministerial portfolios and individual ministers proportionate to the size of their party representation. To implement policies the Cabinet requires cross-community (Protestant and Catholic) support in the assembly via the 'parallel consent formula'. This formula functions in the following way: for a policy to be assented to there must be a majority of both the unionist (Protestant) assembly members and the nationalist (Catholic) assembly members plus a majority of the entire assembly.

At the first meeting of the assembly, David Trimble, then leader of the Protestant UUP, was elected First Minister, and Seamus Mallon of the Catholic SDLP deputy First Minister. However, a lack of agreement between unionist and republican politicians, a perceived failure by the paramilitary groups to decommission weapons and a return to some terrorist activities resulted in the British government suspending the assembly and executive from 14 October 2002 and replacing it once again by direct rule from Westminster. Elections were held to the Northern Ireland Assembly in the following November, but there was no cessation of direct rule.

Conclusion

Devolution has seen the most significant development in the governance of Scotland and Wales for centuries, and Northern Ireland once again has a government, albeit suspended. These developments have been brought about by Tony Blair's Labour government from the late 1990s. One issue which may grow in importance is whether parties in power in Scotland and in Wales develop a policy stance fundamentally at variance with those parties' policies in the Westminster Parliament. We have already seen instances of policy differences in this way, and the question is whether these differences will grow so significantly that friction develops between the parties in Scotland and Wales and those in Westminster. This is not an issue in Northern Ireland, as it has a separate party structure from that for England, Scotland and Wales.

However, local government, apart from London, lacks the powers and a means of finance independent of central government to be truly effective. This raises the question of the value of having local government at all as currently structured.

4

Philosophies and histories of the major political parties

Introduction

The party structure has not changed appreciably since 1945, with the Conservative and Labour Parties alternating in government and the Liberals, now the Liberal Democrats, as the third party. In the 1980s there was a brief period when it looked as though this would change, with the leftward shift of Labour, the creation of the Social Democratic Party as a consequence, and its alliance with the Liberals to create a third force in British politics. But Labour shifted back to the right and the old two-party order returned. Ideologically, however, there was a fundamental change: after 1945 a social democratic consensus developed between the Labour and Conservative Parties, but in the 1980s the Conservatives moved to a neo-liberal agenda and Labour were obliged to do the same to become electable once more. This created a new policy consensus between the main parties.

The major parties and their philosophies

The Conservative Party is the oldest of the principal political parties in Britain. It originated in the 'Tory' faction which emerged in the latter stages of the seventeenth century. Although the Conservative Party's political philosophy became grounded in the work of the eighteenth-century political theorist Edmund Burke and his belief in the maintenance of the institutions of state to ensure order, of the three major parties, the Conservatives have been least influenced by any given ideology. Indeed this has provided the Conservatives with a flexibility which has enabled them to stay in government over a longer period than any other party. In order to understand the Conservative Party one must understand the changing nature of the electorate they have served. The electorate in the eighteenth century consisted of the landed classes, and the philosophy of the Conservative Party evolved to perpetuate and conserve their interests, this being quite consistent with Burke's thinking. To this end they strongly believed both in law and order and in nationalism. Mercantile policy motivated the Conservatives during much of the late eighteenth and nineteenth centuries and this required economic protectionism, imperial expansion and the concomitant expansion in defence forces to police the empire. The exception to this was the recognition by William Pitt the younger of the ascendance of laissez-faire economics; for him this was important as an engine of progress.

The Liberal Party was created on 6 June 1859 from the Whigs (the embryonic Liberals), the Peelites (supporters of Robert Peel, former Prime Minister and creator of the police force) and the Radicals, all of whom opposed the Conservatives. It became a major party of government, alternating in power with the Conservatives for the subsequent sixty years. The Liberal Party evolved to represent the interests of the developing entrepreneurial and managerial classes of the industrial revolution. Their interests were for the free market internally and for free international trade, and this was fundamentally at variance to the economic interests of the landed classes, for whom protected trade forced up food prices and thus land rents. The growing industrial economy and the enlarged franchise enabled the Liberals to enjoy electoral success, but the various Parliamentary Acts to extend the franchise further would cause a fundamental change in philosophy. By the time of the Liberal governments of Henry Campbell-Bannerman (1905–8) and Herbert Asquith (1908–16), policy would be shifting sharply left, although these governments were, if anything, ahead of public opinion in this change.

The Labour Party was initiated in 1900, its formation the result of trade unionists and socialists establishing the Labour Representation Committee, which subsequently evolved into a fully fledged political party under the leadership of James Keir Hardie. However, it would not be until 1924 that it would hold power for the first time, and then in a minority government with James Ramsay MacDonald as party leader and Prime Minister. The Labour Party, evolving from the trades union movement, had a clear socialist philosophy to represent the interests of the proletariat, which meant increased state protection for the workforce against the interests of industry, and increased state expenditure on public service provision, as the working classes received more out of such provision than they contributed to it through taxation. This would be very important as it would explain the growth of government expenditure and thus public services under all governments. The modern vote-buying democracy was thus a product of the franchise extension.

The history of the major parties and the relationships between them

Before 1945

The changes to the franchise in the late nineteenth century presented the Conservatives with a philosophical dilemma: whether to embrace free trade in order to attract the business vote and encourage the pre-eminent position of the British economy, or to address the interests of what was becoming the numerical majority of the working classes, as they were gradually inducted into the franchise. Benjamin Disraeli chose the latter and promoted an inclusive ideology of 'one nation' Conservatism, which would attempt to address working-class interests but present this in a paternalistic way and so not alienate the traditional Conservative voter. This notion would be employed by Conservatives after 1945 to justify their support for the social democratic consensus with the Labour Party on economic and social issues.

The ability of the Labour Party to form its first government in 1924 under Ramsay MacDonald was largely the result of the split in the Liberal Party between the supporters of Asquith and those of David Lloyd George, the latter having displaced the former as Prime Minister in 1916. The Liberals were subsequently kept in power by a coalition with the Conservatives, but once this ended in 1922 the Liberal split would ensure that they would never form a government again. This left a vacuum for those who did not see the Conservatives as promoting their interests, as well as reducing the motivation for the Conservatives to change their position given that their principal political opponent was now neutralised. The working-class vote thus increasingly went to the Labour Party in subsequent years.

Towards the end of the Second World War pressure from the Labour Party meant that the Prime Minister, Winston Churchill, was obliged to call a general election to be held in July 1945. He thus ended the war-time coalition government of Conservatives, Labour and Liberals and headed a brief caretaker Conservative administration while each party fought the general election. Churchill had been temperamentally minded to maintain the coalition after the war, for there had been a continuation of the Lloyd George coalition government after the First World War and a National (coalition)

Government since 1931 because of the Depression, following the Wall Street crash in 1929. Churchill, although considered by many to be a great war-time leader, was not associated with economic and social success in peace-time, and the Conservative Party was largely blamed by the electorate for the economic failures of the 1930s. This led to the Conservatives' second major electoral defeat of the twentieth century (the first being in 1906), being reduced to only 210 MPs.

1945–79

Labour's manifesto for the 1945 election emphasised the poverty experienced by so many in the Depression of the 1930s. The manifesto pledged to eliminate what were known as the 'five evil giants of want, squalor, disease, ignorance and unemployment'. Consequently Labour had a landslide victory, winning 393 seats in the House of Commons. For the first time in its history a Labour government had a majority in the House of Commons and was thus capable of implementing its radical policy programme. The Prime Minister, Clement Attlee, who had been deputy PM in the war-time coalition, was very different from Churchill. Attlee was a clipped and efficient administrator who pushed through policy decisions quickly, whereas Churchill was an orator and great historian of civilisation much prone to rhetoric.

Figure 4.1

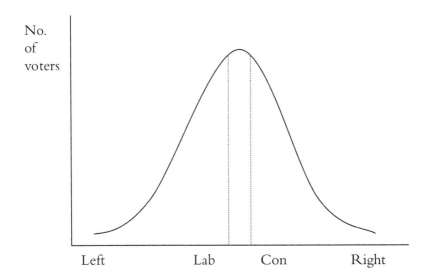

It was thus the experience of high unemployment and the associated social deprivation in the 1930s, plus the perceived success of government intervention in the economy in the Second World War, which caused the electorate to embrace Labour policies on such a large scale in the 1945 election.

To understand this electoral victory more clearly we can employ the median voter theorem. This is a bell-shaped function (see Figure 4.1) with an index of voters on the Y-axis and a simple left–right political spectrum on the X-axis. The assumption is that most voters will support political parties which are in the middle of the spectrum (thus the bell shape of the voter distribution), and if there is no party which represents their views precisely, they will vote for the party which approximates their views most closely. This results in a central clustering of the major political parties as they have to move towards the middle of the political spectrum (the median voter) to attract sufficient votes to form a government (see Figure 4.1).

By 1945 the median voter had moved leftwards (see Figure 4.2) and this meant that a party closer to the right of the spectrum (the Conservatives) could not attract sufficient votes to form a government.

Figure 4.2

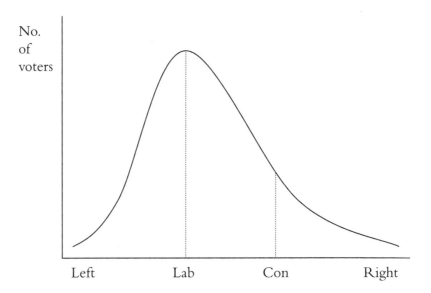

The Labour government had a clear socialist ideology inspiring the domestic economic and social agenda, but adopted the imperialist foreign and colonial policy of its Conservative predecessors and initiated the development of the British atomic bomb, again clearly in line with Conservative defence principles. The government also tried to maintain the Conservative stance on trade protection, although the USA obliged them to alter this. Thus internal policy was socialist, external was conservative.

Early in the century Churchill had switched from the Conservative Party to the Liberals before switching back by the 1920s. Because of his strong links with the Liberal Party he was minded to try and form a political pact with it after the 1945 defeat, but this came to naught. As leader of the opposition between 1945 and 1951, Churchill became largely uninterested in domestic politics, spending his time writing and painting, often abroad.

By 1950 the Labour government had implemented most of its manifesto commitments; indeed, the party appeared to have run out of policy ideas. The general election of that year resulted in Labour's majority in the House of Commons reduced to only five MPs, and the Conservatives skilfully exploited this slim majority. In consequence Attlee dissolved Parliament again in October 1951 and lost the election. Paradoxically, Labour actually gained its highest ever proportion of the aggregate vote (48.8 per cent), but the first-past-the-post electoral system worked against it. Attlee continued as leader of the opposition until 1955, long enough to prevent Herbert Morrison becoming leader. Morrison was seen by many as one of the most significant Labour Party politicians in the post-war government, and indeed in the war-time coalition, having been both Home and Foreign Secretary. He had been a challenger for the Labour Party leadership from 1935, when Attlee had acquired it. Attlee favoured Hugh Gaitskell as his successor, who was more to the right politically and had been Attlee's last Chancellor of the Exchequer (after Stafford Cripps and before him Hugh Dalton). Gaitskell was duly elected as Labour leader and moved policy to the right. However, his untimely death in 1963 led to his succession by Harold Wilson. Wilson, though identified with the left, had positioned himself so as to be acceptable to the right; he would see off the right-wing challenger George Brown and would lead the party to victory in the general election the following year.

The policy stance of the Attlee-led Labour Party created a philosophical problem for the Conservatives: clearly, as the median voter theorem demonstrates, they had to move left to become electable. An acceptance of Labour Party policies on public service issues, state ownership of industries,

trade union involvement in the process of governance and increased government expenditure had to be combined with traditional Conservative policies
on defence, law and order, and fiscal and monetary competence. Churchill
remained rather unenthusiastic about doing this, particularly in respect of the
nationalisation of key industries, but political pragmatism determined by a
vote-buying universal franchise made this policy change necessary.

This movement created a consensus on economic and social policy issues,
as well as on foreign and defence policies. These policies enabled the
Conservatives to regain power in 1951 and then to remain in office
continuously until 1964. Churchill was insistent on staying in office despite
suffering a mild stroke in 1949 and a more serious one in 1953, when his
doctors thought he might die. Whenever people suggested retirement,
Churchill cited William Gladstone, who had formed his last administration as
PM when he was eighty-two. However, in 1955 at the age of eighty Churchill
was forced to retire by his Cabinet in sheer frustration, and the long-time heir
apparent, Anthony Eden, succeeded him. Eden had enormous experience in
foreign affairs: he had been Foreign Secretary during the Second World War
and for a period before it, resigning over the policy of appeasing Nazi
Germany, and resumed the post during Churchill's post-war government.
Yet, incredibly, Eden promptly made a mess of the major foreign policy issue
which he faced as PM, the Suez crisis (see Chapter 12), and was replaced as
Prime Minister by the Chancellor of the Exchequer, Harold Macmillan, in
January 1957.

During this time the greatest leader the Conservatives never had was R. A.
Butler ('Rab' Butler), who came very close to becoming party leader and
Prime Minister on two occasions. He was variously Chancellor of the
Exchequer, Home Secretary and Foreign Secretary in the 1950s and early
1960s and had been Secretary of State for Education in the war-time coalition
government. Most importantly, he had helped define the post-war consensus,
viz. Keynesian macroeconomic policy, a mixed economy with a substantial
number of nationalised industries and the provision of social welfare state
policies. This consensus became known as 'Butskellism', the word being
derived from Butler's name and that of Gaitskell, who had been Chancellor of
the Exchequer prior to Butler taking that office. Butler was on the left of the
Conservative Party, Gaitskell on the right of the Labour Party.

Since 1961 Macmillan's government had been responsible for 'stop–go'
economic policies which led to stagflation (see Chapter 5), and the government had also suffered a high-profile public scandal. The Secretary of State for

War, John Profumo, was discovered to be having a sexual relationship with a prostitute, Christine Keeler, who had also been having a relationship with a Soviet spy. This was the time of the Cuban missile crisis (the attempt by the Soviet Union to install nuclear missiles in Cuba, targeted at the nearby USA), when East–West tensions were at their apogee, and the Profumo scandal was immensely damaging to Macmillan's government. The failure to deal with the stagflating economy caused Macmillan to sack a third of his Cabinet, which became known as the 'night of the long knives'. Macmillan was now politically crippled.

In 1963 Macmillan was diagnosed with cancer and resigned as Prime Minister just as Andrew Bonar Law had done in 1923 in similar circumstances. However, Macmillan had a successful operation and continued to live for a further twenty-three years. But his resignation was fact, and as the Conservative Party determined its leader not by an election but by a consensus among the party grandees, there was confusion concerning Macmillan's successor because of the suddenness of his resignation. As a consequence the Queen was advised to ask Macmillan at his hospital bed who should succeed him. Macmillan did not personally support Butler for the role as Prime Minister and instead proposed the Foreign Secretary, Alec Douglas-Home (then the Earl of Home). This largely unilateral decision upset members of the party and led to the introduction of party elections to decide subsequent Conservative leaders. Douglas-Home, who had to renounce his peerage and win a seat in the House of Commons to be leader, managed to improve the Conservatives' electoral position and they only narrowly lost the 1964 general election.

The ability to renounce a peerage was something new. It was pioneered by the Labour politician Tony Benn. Anthony Wedgwood Benn, to give his full name, was a Labour MP when his father, Viscount Stansgate, died in 1960. As heir, Benn should have inherited this title and moved from the Commons to the Lords, but he refused to do so. There was a court case, and despite attempts to argue that being an aristocrat was 'in the blood', he was eventually able to renounce his title and remain in the Commons.

After 1945 the Liberal Party continued its left-of-centre political stance. This was consistent with the great period of Liberal government in the early part of the century, and the fact that it was a Liberal politician, William Beveridge, in the war-time coalition government who had established the basis of the welfare state. It was also consistent with the leftward shift of the electorate. Jo Grimond led the Liberal Party between 1956 and 1967, during which period the party won several by-elections. The party remained small, however, in terms of its representation in the House of Commons, a fact which would not significantly change until the end of the century.

Let us examine the problem for a third party with the use of the median voter theorem (see Figure 4.3). We can start by considering what happens if the Liberals choose to position themselves in the middle of the political spectrum.

Figure 4.3

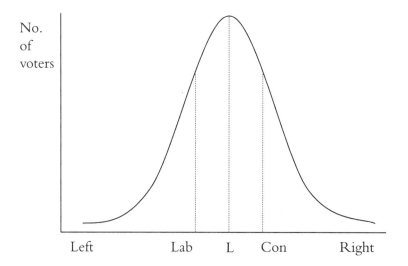

With the Liberals (L) occupying the middle ground they are subject to the 'third-party squeeze'. Labour will attract voters to the left of its position as those voters do not have another party which represents their views and is electable to government. Similarly for the Conservatives on the right. This means that the Liberals will only receive votes from the very centre ground, and this will be insufficient to form a government. By moving to the left of Labour the Liberals attract voters on the left of the political spectrum and put the third-party squeeze on Labour. But why are they then not elected to government? The answer is that the voters do not see the Liberals as electable because they are too small: they have too few seats in Parliament and too small a proportion of the aggregate vote and thus a colossal shift of voters would be needed for them to form a government, and voters think this is unlikely to happen. Voters on the left will thus still mostly vote Labour.

The Conservatives oversaw the completion of economic recovery in the 1950s, and Harold Macmillan was probably accurate when he said during the 1959 general election that the British people had 'never had it so good'. This constituted a philosophical problem for Labour because of the process of *embourgoisement*, meaning that the working classes were becoming richer and therefore aspiring to middle-class values, and demanding policies accordingly. Thus in the 1964 general election Harold Wilson, the Labour Party leader, campaigned, not on socialist ideology, but rather on a technocratic policy of efficient economic management. The electorate were to vote Labour not for ideological reasons but simply because the Labour governing team could manage the modern economy more efficiently than the Conservatives. The approach was successful until it became clear that Labour could not deliver on their promises. Labour's policy programme also addressed social issues relating to the new era of liberalism, with the legalisation of the practices of homosexuality and abortion, legislation making divorce significantly easier, and the lowering of the voting age from twenty-one to eighteen. The government also abolished capital punishment.

The party's majority was increased to ninety-seven in 1966, when Harold Wilson astutely called an early general election while expectations of the Labour government remained high amongst the electorate. With this endorsement, he was able to renationalise the steel industry and introduce comprehensive education. However, the exchange rate crisis of 1967 (see Chapter 5) created a problem in his Cabinet as well as in the country. The Chancellor of the Exchequer, James Callaghan, had repeatedly stated during the mid-1960s that sterling would not be devalued. When eventually the economic fundamentals dictated that it must be, he felt his political position was untenable. So Wilson decided to swap his Chancellor and Home Secretary, making Callaghan Home Secretary and the Home Secretary, Roy Jenkins, Chancellor.

In August 1965 Alec Douglas-Home resigned, and for the first time ever the new leader of the Conservative Party would be elected by a ballot of Conservative MPs. The victor was Edward Heath, whose lower-middle-class background (though he was educated at Balliol College, Oxford) was thought to be more attractive to the electorate than Home's aristocratic background, though Heath's accent and his pastimes of yachting and conducting orchestras hardly conveyed this! Heath continued as Conservative Party leader despite losing the 1966 general election. Four years later, to general surprise, including his own, he won the 1970 general election and became Prime Minister.

In 1968 Heath found himself highly embarrassed by the increasingly radical Conservative politician Enoch Powell, when Powell made an infamous speech claiming that increased immigration would create an ethnic mix which would result in widespread violence, what became known as his 'rivers of blood' speech. Heath was obliged to distance himself from this speech and to sack Powell as a member of the Conservative shadow Cabinet. Powell, who was also opposed to the European Economic Community (EEC), left the Conservative Party early in 1974 and told voters to vote Labour in the February general election when the Labour Party proposed a referendum on EEC membership. Powell went on to join the Ulster Unionist Party and returned to Parliament for a Northern Ireland constituency in the October 1974 election.

Heath was a one-nation Conservative in the tradition of the great nineteenth-century Conservative Prime Minister Benjamin Disraeli. But despite his personal achievement in negotiating Britain's entry to the European Community, the failures of the Heath government's economic, industrial and industrial relations policies (see Chapters 5 and 11) were to beget a radical transformation of the Conservative Party. When Heath called a general election in February 1974 the result was indecisive because the electorate had two main political parties, neither of which had a good technocratic record of economic management. After dallying with the Liberals to try and form a coalition Heath's government fell and was replaced by what would be the last period of tired Labour government with Harold Wilson once again Prime Minister. Wilson would call a second general election in October 1974, which reluctantly gave Labour a bare working majority of three MPs.

Under the leadership of Jeremy Thorpe the Liberal Party enjoyed a significant advance in the 1974 general elections, gaining almost 20 per cent of the aggregate vote. However, there followed a scandal concerning Thorpe and a supposed plot by him to have a homosexual lover murdered. Liberal fortunes dipped as a result. Thorpe consequently resigned as Liberal leader, to be replaced by David Steel.

After losing the two general elections in 1974 Heath was forced to hold a ballot for the party leadership in February 1975, in which he was defeated by Margaret Thatcher, who was far from being a one-nation Tory. The fact that she was a woman was briefly a major issue; she herself had said only a few years before that she did not believe there would be a woman Prime Minister in her lifetime. This issue quickly became of secondary importance.

Harold Wilson retired as PM in 1976 to be replaced by James Callaghan. Wilson was the only Prime Minister since 1945 to retire in office and to do so voluntarily. In consequence, conspiracy theories developed as to why he might have gone. In reality it seems that he was tired of the recurring problems of government and was becoming aware of the early symptoms of Alzheimer's disease; with the worsening economic situation he saw this as a good opportunity to retire as the (then) longest-serving Labour PM ever.

The Labour government of 1974–9 had begun with a small majority and proceeded to lose it through by-election defeats. Callaghan asked the Liberals to support the government, not in a formal coalition but in a pact which became known as the 'Lib–Lab pact'. In return for supporting the government, Steel was able to extract a number of concessions, including an agreement to consult the Liberals on legislation prior to it being introduced in Parliament. The pact collapsed in 1978, and the Liberals did not do well in the general election of 1979.

The Liberals increasingly lobbied for proportional representation (PR) in the House of Commons. The first-past-the-post electoral system meant that their share of the seats in the Commons was always less than their share of the aggregate vote, and PR would correct this. But no major party with a majority in the Commons would want PR as it would reduce their number of seats into line with their aggregate vote. In order to extract PR as a concession from a

Figure 4.4

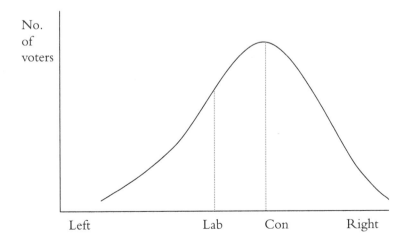

governing party it would be necessary for there to be a hung Parliament and consequently a coalition with the Liberals. The Lib–Lab pact did not last long enough for this to happen, and no hung Parliament has occurred since.

Callaghan, in some measure because he had been a union man, was never able either adequately to see or to deal with the problems of the trade unions, and this led directly to his defeat in the 1979 general election. For some time the electorate had believed that state intervention and growing trade union power were adversely affecting the economy. In terms of the median voter theorem, this had meant a shift in the electorate's beliefs to the right, so the bell-shaped function now offered the most votes to a party of the right (see Figure 4.4). Margaret Thatcher's policies would be consistent with this rightward shift in the electorate's beliefs.

1979 and after

Thatcher was the first ideologically motivated PM since Clement Attlee left office in 1951. She approached economic governance with the philosophy of the Liberal Party of the nineteenth century rather than with a Conservative philosophy, and she established a neo-liberal economic agenda which became orthodoxy. Her policy of reversing relative economic decline via the free market was, however, combined with traditional Conservative policies on defence, law and order, fiscal and monetary competence and a belief in the inviolable sovereignty of the state. So her philosophy was neo-liberal in economic matters, but traditionally Conservative in others. These policies were combined with a centralising of the state apparatus, done in order to promote the policy agenda of the core executive more effectively. Vested interests such as the trade unions were excluded from the policy formation process, and special advisors to government would marginalise the civil service. The virtue of such strong government was seen and would be subsequently implemented by Tony Blair. Thus a new period of consensus on major policy themes would be established between the two parties of government.

Thatcher was a factional leader who never sought compromise, but drove her transforming policies through with vigour. She led the Conservatives to three successive general election victories in 1979, 1983 and 1987, during which she transformed the British economy and had a significant influence internationally. She was vigorously opposed by many one-nation Conservatives of her own party, including Edward Heath, who never forgave her for replacing him, and for her hostile policies towards the EEC.

Voters elect parties of government principally on the basis of their leader's appearances on television. Thatcher recognised the need for personal presentational qualities. To this end, she had her hair restyled, would 'power dress', as became the fashion for women in the 1980s, and received voice-training lessons to lower the register of her voice.

With Labour heavily defeated in the 1979 election, the party began an internal debate about policy. Michael Foot, the veteran left-winger, was elected Labour leader in 1981 and proceeded to develop the most left-wing manifesto a Labour Party had fielded since 1945. The rightward shift of the electorate ensured that this was a suicidal policy stance; indeed the manifesto became known as the 'longest political suicide note in history'.

There were some Labour politicians who were not prepared to remain in the party given this change, and this led to the forming of a breakaway group, the Social Democratic Party (SDP) in 1981, founded by a former Chancellor of the Exchequer, Roy Jenkins; a former Foreign Secretary, David Owen; a former Secretary of State for Education, Shirley Williams; and a former Secretary of State for Transport, William Rodgers. The SDP was led initially by Jenkins and later by Owen. To avoid the adverse electoral consequences of two centrist parties competing with one another, an alliance (as their cooperation became known) was forged between the SDP and the Liberals, the latter still being led by David Steel. In the 1983 general election the Alliance received 25 per cent of the aggregate vote, while the Labour Party performed catastrophically, receiving just 27.6 per cent, their lowest since 1918. Following a fall in their electoral support in the 1987 general election, a majority in both the SDP and Liberal parties voted in 1988 for a formal merger, and the Social and Liberal Democratic Party, known from 1989 as the Liberal Democratic Party (or Lib Dems), was formed. The leader, Paddy Ashdown, was inherited from the Liberals.

The Labour Party was now obliged to move right to attract votes away from the Conservatives (see Figure 4.4), and so, just as the Conservatives had had to ditch part of their philosophy after the Labour victory of 1945, now Labour had to do the same in the 1980s. *Embourgoisement* was Labour's critical problem. The majority of the British people had become richer during the 1980s and Labour had to adopt the Thatcher philosophy on the economy to become electable. Switching policies and convincing the electorate takes time, and this would not be achieved until 1997, with the help of policy errors by the Conservatives. There was no ideological difference on the substantive issues in the 1997 general election between Labour and the Conservatives; rather, once again Labour would campaign on the issue of technocracy.

Michael Foot was replaced by Neil Kinnock as Labour Party leader in 1983. Kinnock marginalised the extreme left within the party, particularly the group known as Militant, and shifted policy to the right. Presentational issues would be handled by a new Campaigns and Communications Directorate under Peter Mandelson. Mandelson's influence on policy development and efficient manipulation of the media would eventually help to transform Labour. Despite this Labour still lost the 1987 election by a substantial margin and a further policy shift to the right was deemed necessary. Unilateral nuclear disarmament, high direct taxation and the nationalisation of major industries were all abandoned in a new policy document called 'Meet the Challenge, Make the Change'.

At the end of the 1980s the senior members of the Conservative Party were becoming increasingly fed up with Margaret Thatcher's hectoring style of stewardship. What had seemed necessary in the early days of her leadership, when so many policy changes were needed and so many vested interests in society required radical reform, now seemed a liability. The party increasingly believed that the electorate were taking the same view. This led directly to Thatcher's defeat in a leadership ballot in November 1990. The ballot, which was precipitated by Michael Heseltine, a one-nation Tory and long-time opponent of Thatcher, also included the Foreign Secretary, Douglas Hurd, and the Chancellor of the Exchequer, John Major. The victor was Major, the candidate thought most able to unify a divided party as he was not identified with any faction. His government achieved a small majority in the general election of April 1992.

The 1992 general election would result in Labour's fourth successive election defeat and Kinnock was replaced by John Smith. Smith continued the process of shifting policy to the right and reducing left-wing influence in leadershp decisions, and to this end he engaged in reform of the trade union block vote. This is where the leadership of unions affiliated to the Labour Party significantly influence policy decisions at Labour conferences by wielding a block vote determined by their membership size. However, increasingly, the Labour Party leadership takes little notice of the conference decisions anyway!

Prior to the early 1980s Labour Party leaders were elected by the Parliamentary Labour Party (the Labour MPs). This was then changed so that Labour MPs, constituency party members and trade unions in three equal measures decided the leadership. At the 1993 party conference Smith won a conference vote to introduce the one member, one vote (OMOV) system for selecting parliamentary candidates. But the leadership election system remained unchanged.

Immediately after the 1992 election the Conservative government became embroiled in a sterling crisis which led to ejection from the European Monetary System, the day on which this happened becoming known as 'Black Wendesday' (see Chapter 5). For Labour this resulted in major electoral gains in the 1994 local elections. However, early in the morning of 12 May 1994 John Smith suffered a fatal heart attack. Thirty-one years before the Labour Party had suffered the death of its leader, Hugh Gaitskell, shortly before it returned to government. The consequent leadership contest saw the election of Tony Blair, the youngest ever leader of the Labour Party.

John Major inaugurated a 'back to basics' campaign which attempted to signify a return to core Conservative policies. This was interpreted by the media as signifying high standards of sexual morality and financial probity, and when a number of more senior Conservatives were found wanting in this regard, the media accused the Tories of being embroiled in 'sleaze', thus the policy backfired spectacularly. This, combined with the exchange rate crisis, a brief period of economic recession which caused a fall in Conservative support in southern England and party disunity, resulted in growing opposition to Major from within his own party. Major consequently called a leadership election to try and quell this. Michael Portillo, the defence secretary, and seen by some as the heir to Thatcher, started to mount a challenge, but one of the potentially strong candidates, Michael Heseltine, had already done a deal with Major where he would not stand as a contender in return for being appointed deputy Prime Minister. It was this deal which had prompted Major to call the leadership election in the first place, and challenge to his leadership quickly fell away in consequence. However, opposition from the national electorate was at fever pitch and at the general election on 1 May 1997 the Conservatives suffered a landslide defeat. Conservative representation was down to only 165 MPs, and Major at once resigned as party leader. This was one of three landslide defeats the Conservatives suffered in the twentieth century (the other two being in 1906 and 1945). The party replaced Major with William Hague, its youngest leader in modern history.

In the 1992 general election the Liberal Democrats won twenty seats with 18.3 per cent of the aggregate vote, but in the 1997 election they gained forty-six seats, their largest representation in the Commons and largest in the history of the Liberals since before the Second World War, although they only received 17.3 per cent of the aggregate vote. Paddy Ashdown led the party in both elections. The fact that the Conservative vote had slumped constituted a tactical dilemma for the Liberal Democrats: whether to attempt to replace the Conservatives as the main opposition party, or whether to maintain their stance as a left-of-centre party. Despite the seductive nature of the former strategy, and its backing by the party's new leader (from 1999), Charles Kennedy, they adopted the latter to attract the Labour vote. However, Liberal Democrat candidates present different political messages to constituents depending upon their principal opponents (Conservative or Labour) in each constituency!

The ideological notion of the 'third way' became central to Tony Blair's policies. The hyperbole gave the impression that this was a new ideology which transcended the old left/right political split and would constitute the primary political ideology of the post-Cold War world. In reality, when the Blair government was elected, there was no appreciable change in polices from the neo-liberal philosophy of the Thatcher–Major years.

Tony Blair continued the rightward shift of Labour Party policy, advocating the re-writing of Clause 4 of the party's constitution, thereby dropping the commitment to nationalising the commanding heights of the economy. Blair and his team managed to ensure substantial support for the proposal within the party despite opposition from the left. In 1996 the draft manifesto 'New Labour, New Life for Britain' was published, which the leadership ensured was fully costed to avoid Conservative claims that Labour would have to raise taxes substantially. It was supported by 95 per cent of the party. In the 1997 general election the Labour Party won a landslide victory with 418 MPs, which included a record 101 women. Labour had a majority of 179.

The Conservatives under Hague decided to address the division in the party over European unification, not by compromise, as Major had attempted and failed to do, but by adopting a clearly 'Euro-sceptic' policy, ruling out joining the single European currency, the euro. This deepened the divide in the party; however, in the elections to the European Parliament in June 1999 the Conservatives doubled their representation to thirty-six seats. But concentration on the single currency was a profound mistake in the 2001 general election. The Liberal Democrats showed in their private polling that the electorate rated the issue only thirteenth in order of priority.

On 7 June 2001 Tony Blair led the Labour Party to a second successive landslide victory in a general election with a majority of 167. Only 166 Conservative MPs were elected, just one more than in 1997, and on the morning after the election Hague resigned. Apart from policy issues Hague lacked the physical stature increasingly required by successful statesmen in the television age.

The Conservative Party had introduced a new election system for the leadership: a ballot of Conservative MPs would determine two leading candidates, and the party membership would then vote to choose a winner. The party membership, renowned for its right-wing and anti-European stance, was faced with the left-of-centre pro-Europe former Chancellor of the Exchequer Kenneth Clarke as one candidate, and the little-known right-wing anti-European MP Iain Duncan Smith as the other. In September 2001 the membership voted for the latter by a substantial margin.

The Conservatives supported Blair's policy of regime change in Iraq during the spring and summer of 2003 (see Chapter 12), which was consistent with Conservative thinking although the Labour Party remained deeply divided on the issue. The Liberal Democrats, and particularly their leader, Charles Kennedy, opposed this policy and they would see further advances in their number of MPs in the 2005 general election (sixty-two seats and 22 per cent of the aggregate vote) over and above their advances in the 2001 election (fifty-two seats and 18.3 per cent of the aggregate vote).

A significant minority of Conservative MPs had been opposed to Duncan Smith's leadership from the outset, and the continued low opinion poll ratings caused this number to increase during the summer and autumn of 2003. Duncan Smith lacked the necessary presentational qualities of a statesman, as well as lacking a grip on policy issues and the organisational structure of the party. This lack of support within his own party culminated in a ballot of Conservative MPs on 29 October 2003, in which Duncan Smith was sacked as leader by seventy-five votes to ninety. Because the party feared that this disunity over the leadership would be electorally damaging, the former Home Secretary Michael Howard was able to persuade the party not to have a leadership election but simply to nominate one candidate to replace Duncan Smith, himself. Thus on 6 November Howard was declared leader. He was an older and more experienced politician than both of his predecessors, having been a Cabinet minister from 1990 to 1997. Most importantly, he exercised a remarkably firm grip on the party apparatus and fired even senior members of his party when they made public comments at variance with the party line.

At the 2005 general election the Labour Party alleged that the Tories would cut public expenditure substantially. The Conservatives, however, wanted to talk principally about immigration and crime. On 5 May 2005, for the first time in its history, Labour achieved a third consecutive term in government, albeit with a vastly reduced majority of sixty-seven.

The Conservatives faced a fundamental dilemma in philosophy. If they adopted the technocratic policy of Labour, given their own poor performance in government and while Labour appeared to be managing the economy well, why should the electorate vote Conservative when they already had a government with this philosophy which appeared to be performing efficiently? On the other hand, if the Conservatives adopted a more traditional Conservative philosophy then they would alienate the proportion of the electorate who are economically reliant upon the Labour spending policies and would probably attract no portion of the electorate they were not already attracting in general elections.

Howard resigned as Conservative Party leader after the 2005 general election on the grounds that he would be too old to lead the party into the subsequent general election. He remained as caretaker leader while he attempted and failed to change the leadership contest rules to return the decision to Conservative MPs. A number of candidates put themselves forward including the old guard represented by Kenneth Clarke and former Foreign Secretary Malcolm Rifkind. But the two candidates who went through to the run off for the party membership to decide were the right-wing candidate David Davis and the Blair clone David Cameron. At just thirty-nine years of age and with no more than five years in Parliament and no experience in government, Cameron won in December 2005. Clearly the Conservatives had decided that adopting a largely New Labour policy stance was necessary to be electable, that is, shifting left as close to Labour as they could to increase their vote according to the median voter theorem, and that Cameron would appeal to the voters on a technocratic ticket.

In December 2005 Charles Kennedy was forced to resign as Liberal Democrat leader over revelations that he was an alcoholic. The subsequent leadership campaign reopened the conundrum as to whether the Liberal Democrats should face left to Labour or right to the Conservatives, though they denied seeing it in those terms. In March 2006 Sir Menzies Campbell was elected, representing the left wing of the party, but not before harm had been done to the party's reputation and appeal to voters by the revelations about Kennedy, but also to some extent by the admission of one of the failed leadership candidates, Simon Hughes, that he was bisexual, and most particularly by the revelation of the use of male prostitutes by another of the failed leadership candidates, Mark Oaten, who was married with children.

Tony Blair and his Chancellor of the Exchequer, Gordon Brown, had a tacit agreement that the former would resign and hand over power as PM to the latter in due course. Blair entered his third term in office without so doing, and this caused friction between the two which constituted an impediment to efficient government. It is also the reason why when Blair periodically reshuffled his cabinet, he did not feel able to shift Brown from the Treasury, as this would enhance that friction. This has resulted in Brown being one of the longest serving Cabinet ministers in the one capacity in history.

Conclusion

Two-party politics is clearly entrenched: the party machines of the Conservatives and Labour and their historical legacies have continued to ensure that they are the only realistic parties of government. Ideologically there was a sharp shift to the left on economic, social and industrial policy by the Labour Party at the end of the Second World War, which was followed reluctantly by the Conservative Party, and a long period of consensus ensued between them on the major policy themes. The consensus was fundamentally broken by Margaret Thatcher, who took the Conservatives on a sharp rightward shift in the late 1970s. Labour was reluctantly obliged to follow, though this took many years finally to accomplish. However, there has been a gradual shift to the left by both parties in the first few years of the twenty-first century. As the gap between the major parties narrows, some commentators believe that there could be a hung Parliament at the next general election, increasing the importance of the Liberal Democrats.

5

Macroeconomic policies

Introduction

There have been two distinct phases of macroeconomic policy since 1945. In the first, up until approximately 1977, successive governments managed Britain's relative economic decline vis-à-vis the world's major industrial nations. During this period polices were based on the theories of the great British economist John Maynard Keynes. The second phase was where policies were based on the theories of the American economist Milton Friedman. The performance of the macroeconomy improved as Germany and Japan stagnated, and Britain overtook France to become the fourth largest economy in the world.

The first phase

After the Second World War, there existed a consensus between the major political parties in Britain regarding the appropriate macroeconomic policy. It was the Cambridge economist John Maynard Keynes who would be the architect of these policies, though his death in 1946 would ensure that he was never to see their consequences. The policies were prompted by the experience of the Wall Street crash of 1929, and the consequent high unemployment in the Depression of the 1930s. The principal policy between 1945 and approximately 1977 was to maintain full employment by fiscal demand management, in other words the use of government expenditure and taxation to control aggregate demand and so employment.

Prior to the Second World War, British governments employed classical economic theory: the expectation that the economy was always at the full employment level of national income because of free markets that cleared perfectly. Classical economics requires governments to prevent monopolies, to prevent trade union restrictions upon labour market clearing and to maintain the gold standard. The latter was suspended for a while from the First World War, and finally abandoned in 1931 because of the Depression.

However, the classical model had already been vitiated by the policies of the reforming Liberal governments before the First World War which extended trade union rights, introduced statutory minimum wages in major industries (see Chapter 11) and introduced unemployment and sickness benefits (see Chapter 6). All of these measures prevented the classical economic polices from working efficiently as they created nominal wage 'stickiness'. As wages constitute a high proportion of the total costs of a business, output prices became 'sticky' as well. This means that the wage–price adjustment mechanism did not function according to free-market forces, in other words, as demand and supply conditions changed in the employment market, wages did not respond freely to such changes. This also means that output prices did not respond freely to changes in aggregate demand either, and thus the economy did not naturally equilibrate at full employment.

In the Depression of the 1930s markets were not clearing properly according to classical principles and unemployment was consequently high. As the public wanted all of the social legislation which prevented the classical policies from working efficiently, a solution to achieve full employment which did not require reversing social policy legislation was going to find favour. In consequence John Maynard Keynes's theories increasingly appeared to provide a policy solution to unemployment. Keynes showed that in this economic environment governments could raise aggregate demand by using fiscal policy (government expenditure and taxation) and by so doing create full employment. We shall examine how and why such a policy functioned.

Keynes had argued that the demand for money (or liquidity) is very elastic and indeed infinitely elastic at low levels of interest – everybody demands their wealth in the form of cash rather than in interest-earning accounts (the 'liquidity trap'). This means that even large changes in the money supply will cause only small changes in the interest rate. Keynes also argued that investment decisions are largely determined by expectations of future demand, and not by the interest rate. This means that any fall in the interest rate will have only a minimal effect upon investment decisions. These two facts mean that the monetary transmission mechanism is vitiated and thus monetary policy (the Bank of England's control of the supply of money and the interest rate) is rendered ineffective (see Figure 5.1).

However, Keynes argued that just as this causes monetary policy to be

Figure 5.1

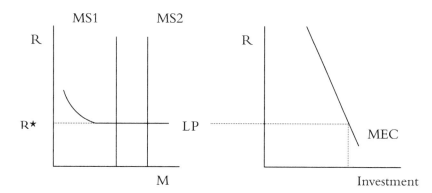

Keynes's interpretation of the money market is illustrated in the left hand diagram. This has the interest rate (R) on the Y-axis and the quantity of money (M) measured on the X-axis. Keynes's term for the demand for money was liquidity preference (LP). Assume the money supply is MS1 *ab initio*, and that the Bank of England now increases the money supply to MS2, but as we can see the interest rate will remain constant at R★, what Keynes called the 'liquidity trap'. In the right hand diagram the investment function (the demand for capital equipment by businesses) is illustrated, or as Keynes called it the Marginal Efficiency of Capital (MEC). The function is quite steep showing that even large changes in the interest rate won't change investment much. If the interest rate can't change much, or indeed at all because of the liquidity trap, then investment won't change with monetary policy and so output and employment in the economy won't change either.

ineffective, it causes fiscal policy to be very effective. A fiscal expansion by the government (namely increased public expenditure and/or reduced taxation) will cause large changes in national income and thus employment, because there is very little crowding out of interest-sensitive private expenditure. What this means is that because of the liquidity trap, a fiscal expansion will not tend to drive the interest rate up, and so investment will not fall much in consequence of such a fiscal expansion, and so will not tend to offset that expansion. A fiscal expansion can be achieved by either increasing government expenditure or decreasing taxation, or both, the difference between expenditure and tax receipts being financed through government borrowing (deficit financing). There is also a multiplier effect on the economy of this policy as increased expenditure on businesses by government or by consumers will cause them to spend more on buying component parts, and the suppliers of these parts will in turn spend more on raw materials and so forth.

The classical model, with fully flexible wages and prices and so with all markets clearing, causes the economy to be at full employment. This means that national output or aggregate supply is fixed by the magnitude of full employment, and so the aggregate supply curve is vertical. In this case changes in aggregate demand by fiscal policy will not change output and employment,

Figure 5.2

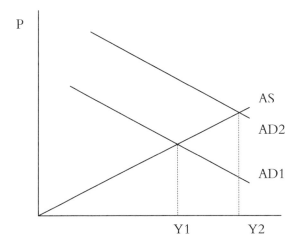

This illustrates the aggregate market for all goods and services in the economy; prices, P are on the Y-axis, and National output, Y is on the X-axis. With wages and prices sticky the Aggregate Supply curve (AS) slopes gently upwards. This means that when government increases Aggregate Demand (AD1 to AD2) by increasing government expenditure or reducing taxation then output will rise (Y1 to Y2) and unemployment will fall as firms demand more labour to produce the additional goods.

but with sticky wages and prices the aggregate supply curve is not vertical, but relatively elastic (flat), and now fiscal policy can be used to change aggregate demand and therefore output and employment (see Figure 5.2).

The electorate could clearly remember the exceptional unemployment of the Depression and the associated social deprivation. What they feared was that once demand for military materiel declined at the end of the war there would be a return to the economic and social experiences of the 1930s. As a consequence, in the 1945 election campaign, the Labour Party promised that full employment would constitute the principal macroeconomic objective and Keynesian demand management was to be the instrument by which this objective would be maintained. In order to exercise further control over the economy, the Labour government nationalised the Bank of England in 1946.

In fact, after the Second World War, apart from a brief period during demobilisation, there were labour shortages, not unemployment, to deal with. In the immediate post-war period the employment shortage problem was partially addressed by a protracted system of repatriating German prisoners of war (PoWs), of which some 400,000 had been amassed during wartime. Many of these PoWs were used to work in the British economy at low cost to the state. The final repatriations were not completed until 1948. By the 1950s the labour shortages were reduced as the result of immigration from the Caribbean and from other British dependent territories, augmented in the 1960s by immigration from the Indian sub-continent. In addition to the macroeconomic effects of providing labour to undertake low-wage employment, and the benefits of the entrepreneurialism of some of the immigrants, the immigration would alter the ethnic mix of British society in a fundamental way.

The initial problem for fiscal policy in 1945 was the fact that Britain was in effect bankrupt, a result of fighting six years of total war. The USA scrapped President Roosevelt's policy of lend-lease immediately after the end of the war. This policy involved the US providing Britain with considerable material resources to prosecute the war in return for the lease of assets such as military bases throughout the Empire. With the ending of this policy, Britain needed to borrow heavily from the US, and a $3.75 billion loan was provided at interest in the autumn of 1945, to be repaid over fifty years. Subsequently Britain was in receipt of nearly a quarter of the $13 billion of Marshall Aid from the US, the rest being received by other western European countries and Japan. This was grant aid provided by the US to rebuild the economies of those countries under American hegemony, and formed part of the Truman doctrine. This doctrine was to contain Soviet expansionism and so prevent Soviet influence in countries under American hegemony. Through the rapid economic reconstruction of western Europe and Japan, it was expected that the electorate of these countries would vote for politically moderate governments, and so create a bulwark against influence by communist or other extremist political movements.

However, much of the finance which Britain received from the US was used to fund the policing of the empire, and so retain Britain's position as a superpower. To some extent, paradoxically, this was consistent with American policy, as it reduced the role the Americans needed to play in containing the Soviet Union globally.

Exchange rate policy was determined by Keynesian theory, and by the reality of post-war American hegemony. Keynes was fully aware that with a degree of price stickiness a fixed exchange rate regime and controls on capital movements across the exchanges was required to enable his demand management policies to function. This was because increases in aggregate demand through the use of expansionary fiscal policy would otherwise tend to raise the interest rate, attract inflows of capital into the economy as a result, and so raise the exchange rate. This in turn would cause exports to fall and imports to rise and so aggregate demand would fall back to where it had started prior to the fiscal expansion, so no beneficial expansion to the economy would have taken place. Thus Keynes was broadly supportive of the American-sponsored post-war Bretton Woods 'fixed' exchange rate system.* The US had learned from the inter-war years, when economic collapse led to political extremism in Europe, and wished to introduce the Bretton Woods system in order to create a stable economic environment to facilitate post-war growth in international trade. To this end the US also created the General Agreement on Tariffs and Trade (GATT), part of the United Nations, which would result in reduced trade protectionism (in 1995 GATT was replaced by the World Trade Organization). The result of these measures was to increase economic inter-dependence, which in turn led to increased political inter-dependence among countries under American hegemony, and secured rapid economic growth and so political stability.

Britain entered Bretton Woods at a dollar–sterling exchange rate of $4.03 to the pound. This was an error of judgement, for although this was lower than the pre-First World War parity, the competitiveness of British industry had eroded significantly in the interim and so sterling was over-valued at this rate. Because of this over-valuation, the convertibility of sterling into other currencies resulted in it being sold on the foreign exchange markets, and so full convertibility had to be suspended in 1947 and sterling had to be devalued to $2.80 in 1949 as a consequence. With labour shortages after the war,

---

*The Bretton Woods exchange rate system was not perfectly fixed, as currencies fluctuated within a band; and it was an adjustable peg system in which currencies could be periodically revalued.

Keynesian fiscal demand management was used more to constrain domestic demand, in order to maintain the exchange rate, than to boost employment. This worked in the following manner: keeping taxes high kept down inflation, which stopped the erosion of trade competitiveness, and constraining the domestic economy reduced the demand for imports, so if the trade balance does not deteriorate then sterling does not fall.

With loans to be repaid and a fixed exchange rate system, the Attlee government had a policy of export-led recovery, and this meant that the domestic rationing of consumer products, which had begun in 1940 because of the war, did not end until 1954. As a consequence much domestic production was directed at export, significantly to the USA (which was the only country to come out of the Second World War richer than it went in) and subsequently to western Europe, where the economy was recovering largely because of the 'German economic miracle' (the rapid post-war recovery of the West German economy). This policy began the gradual process of economic recovery in Britain, and earned foreign currency to pay off foreign debt.

The Attlee government had wanted to retain its 'imperial preference' trade policy after the war. Imperial preference had been proposed by the Conservative politician Joseph Chamberlain half a century earlier; it was effectively a customs union to protect British Empire trade and was a response to the erection of trade barriers by other industrial countries. It was not passed into law at the time, but one of his sons, Neville Chamberlain, when Chancellor of the Exchequer, introduced it in 1932 under the name of the 'general tariff' because of the Depression. Maintaining these trade links, it was thought, would keep the Empire bound to Britain and would act as a deterrent to the influence of the USSR. Keynes argued that restricted trade would insulate Britain from demand shocks and thus enable policies based on his theories to promote economic growth more effectively. However, the American policy of free trade was inconsistent with the British system of protectionism, and so in return for the substantial post-war loan, the US forced Britain to make serious trade concessions. On 1 January 1948 the Geneva round of GATT was completed, where Britain was obliged under American hegemony to participate in a reduction of trade barriers.

With the return of Winston Churchill as Conservative PM in 1951, the macroeconomic paradigm was now set. Keynesian demand management became largely apolitical, as it was consistent with either a predominantly free-market economy or one with a high degree of nationalisation. It was now generally accepted as the new economic orthodoxy. During much of the subsequent thirteen years of continuous Conservative government, the post-war economic recovery continued, with unemployment low and debt being repaid. By the time of the 1959 general election, the then Prime Minister, Harold Macmillan, famously said the British people 'had never had it so good'. He was duly re-elected. However, by the early 1960s the Macmillan government was employing what came to be known as 'stop–go' macro-economic policy. This was expansionary policy to stimulate the economy followed by contractionary policy to choke off the inflation generated and to maintain the exchange rate. This caused the beginnings of stagflation, and was to help Labour to power in 1964.

However, productivity in the British economy continued to lag behind that of the US and West Germany (see Chapter 11), but Keynesian demand management policy has no beneficial effect on productivity. Rather there was a return to the 'stop–go' macroeconomic policy which had plagued the last days of the Macmillan government. Because the expansionary phase of this policy raised domestic prices and created increased demand for imports and because of the relative lack of productivity in the British economy, this led to a balance-of-payments deficit in the fixed exchange rate system. This in turn eventually led to the exchange rate crisis of 1967, when the value of the pound was reduced to $2.40. This had considerable political implications for the government of the time, led by Harold Wilson, as the need to devalue was interpreted by the electorate as political mismanagement, and was one reason for his government losing the 1970 general election.

By the end of the 1960s it was increasingly clear that the USA was becoming both unwilling and unable to maintain currency stability. The countries in the European Economic Community therefore decided to set up a system called the 'snake in the tunnel', where EEC currencies would have a narrow fluctuation band (the 'snake') but continue to operate within the Bretton Woods system (the 'tunnel'). Currency bands for EEC countries were consequently devised (principally the narrow 1.125% band), but when the Bretton Woods system effectively collapsed in 1971 these proposed bands were scrapped. After the US-sponsored Smithsonian agreement of 1972 it was decided that European currencies should operate within a 2.25% snake, while they would fluctuate against the dollar in a wider tunnel. Sterling was a member of this system but was ejected in 1972 because of heavy selling on the foreign exchange markets. Britain consequently moved to a flexible exchange rate regime, which resulted in sterling periodically depreciating through the 1970s.

Unemployment and inflation, or stagflation, was growing by the end of the 1960s, largely as the result of British industry being less productive than that of the US, West Germany and other countries. These productivity inefficiencies were causing businesses to raise prices to consumers, which in turn stimulated trade union demands for increased wages, thus generating a wage–price spiral. Employing Keynesian demand management policy was problematic as Keynesian theory had conflicting policy prescriptions for unemployment and inflation: for unemployment the fiscal stance was to be expanded, while for inflation it was to be contracted. As a consequence it was to be the rival 'monetarist' theory which would start to influence policy.

In 1971–2 the Chancellor of the Exchequer, Anthony Barber, under Conservative Prime Minister Edward Heath, expanded both the money supply as well as government expenditure to deal with growing unemployment in what became known as the 'Barber boom'. Between 1971 and 1973 the effect of the monetary expansion was to see bank lending rise from £71 million to £1,332 million. However, this monetary expansion was the very opposite policy to that prescribed by the monetarists in an inflationary environment. Consequently the policy caused a growth in inflation and it was reversed: the notorious U-turn.

Heath's government also introduced wage and pay freezes to try to deal with the inflationary problem, which was significantly worsened by the first OPEC oil price rise of 1973–4. OPEC, the Organization of the Petroleum Exporting Countries, initiated this strategy so as to increase income to its member states, which were largely developing countries in the Middle East and elsewhere. However, unemployment in Britain, which had exceeded one million in 1972 for the first time since the Depression of the 1930s, was back down to about 600,000 by the end of Heath's ministry.

In 1975, the Wilson Labour government had another go at corporatism (a tripartite agreement between government, unions and businesses concerning wages and prices), which had been used in the 1960s (see Chapter 11) to address the wage–price spiral. The Trades Union Congress agreed with the government and the Confederation of British Industry to a flat-rate pay rise together with price controls and improvements in welfare spending. This became known as the 'social contract' and, as with previous corporatist agreements, was short lived, for in 1976, with inflation at 24 per cent, sterling was sold heavily on the foreign exchange markets. There was a balance-of-payments crisis and the Labour government had to turn, reluctantly, to the International Monetary Fund for a loan to pay government debt and to prevent further falls in the exchange rate. The price the government was obliged to pay was the reduction of government expenditure and a contractionary monetary policy. The Chancellor of the Exchequer, Denis Healey, had to some extent anticipated this as he had already cut public expenditure. Healey had one other claim to fame as Chancellor, the introduction of the term 'public sector borrowing requirement' (PSBR) to refer to government borrowing.

In 1977 OPEC again raised oil prices substantially, which rapidly increased both unemployment and inflation in the developed world. Britain and other industrial countries were now stagflating significantly, a problem for which Keynesian demand management policy has no prescription, as we have seen. By 1977 unemployment had grown to 1.42 million. At this time James Callaghan was Labour Prime Minister; he was an old trade union-based politician and at first he was reluctant to abandon traditional socialist (interventionist) policy. However, there was some sign of the paradigm shift from Keynesian policy to monetarist policy during his premiership, when he publicly stated that the old Keynesian policies were no longer tenable.

This contractionary monetary policy which Britain was obliged to employ was also employed by the G7 countries (the seven largest economies in the world) to deal with inflation, and this was combined with an expansionary fiscal policy to deal with unemployment. But the failure to make the complete paradigm shift to monetarism, instead combining Keynesian and monetarist policies, was theoretically incoherent. Keynesian theory assumed nominal variables (namely money wages, prices and the nominal interest rate) were largely constant; monetarist theory assumed they were not. Moreover, the foregoing combination of policies had contradictory effects, the expansionary fiscal policy reducing unemployment and increasing inflation and the contractionary monetary policy the opposite.

The combination of the OPEC action, strikes and a lack of effective macroeconomic management led both to the three-day week in the winter of 1973–4, when the Heath government restricted industrial production to three days a week because of power shortages, and to the 'winter of discontent' in the winter of 1978–9, when the Callaghan government was faced with massive strike action. In both cases these events led to the collapse of their respective governments (see also Chapter 11).

The second phase

High unemployment enabled Margaret Thatcher to become Prime Minister in 1979. She had become leader of the Conservative Party in 1975, and in the intervening four years had developed a macroeconomic policy to be implemented when in government. This policy abandoned Keynesian demand management, and it abandoned the principal policy objective of full employment. Instead the principal policy objective was to be the maintenance of stable prices, and monetary policy was to be employed as the instrument to achieve it. The monetarist theories of Milton Friedman were now used as the basis of macroeconomic policy. The complete paradigm shift from Keynesian theory to monetarism had been made.

Friedman argued that it was the use of Keynesian policy to expand the economy to increase employment and then contract the economy to deal with the resulting inflation which was causing stagflation. The relationship between inflation and unemployment had been illustrated by the 'Phillips curve', devised by A. W. Phillips some years previously (a simple inverse relationship – as the economy grows unemployment falls and inflation rises; as the economy contracts, the opposite occurs). Friedman realised that this relationship was more complex than the original curve illustrated, and so he developed the 'expectations-augmented Phillips curve'. He argued that in the long run any inflation rate was consistent with a given rate of unemployment, so the 'long-run Phillips curve' (LRPC) was vertical (see Figure 5.3). Only in the short run is the relationship between inflation and unemployment inversely correlated as the original Phillips curve had showed, so Friedman referred to this as the 'short-run Phillips curve' (SRPC). The latter will move up or down as the expected inflation rate rises or falls respectively.

Let us assume that the economy starts at point A in Figure 5.3 and is then expanded by the government as they approach the next general election in order to please the electorate, and so it moves to B. Unemployment has fallen but inflation has risen. The government keeps expanding the economy and the SRPC moves up from SRPC1 to SRPC2 as the expected rate of inflation increases and the economy moves to C. The government is either re-elected or the opposition party is elected and the new government has to deal with the inflation, and so contracts the economy. The economy now moves to point D as a result. This is a stagflating economy; we can see this by comparing point D with point A (where we started). Both inflation and unemployment are higher at D than at A.

Figure 5.3

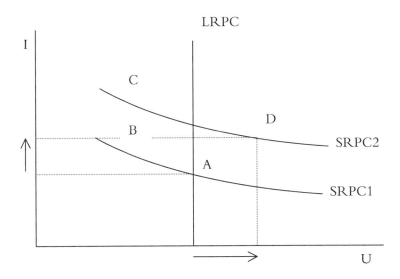

Inflation (I), is on the Y-axis, and unemployment (U) on the X-axis. Each short-run Phillips Curve (SRPC) illustrates a trade-off between inflation and unemployment. In the short run governments, by expanding the economy, can have less of the latter only at the expense of more of the former. In the long-run unemployment is determined by the long-run Phillips curve (LRPC). The government will want to expand the economy to be re-elected. Assume the economy is at point A *ab initio* and the government then expands the economy and thus moves to B, where there is more inflation but less unemployment; if the government keeps expanding the economy the short-run Phillips curve moves up (SRPC1 to SRPC2) as the expected inflation rate increases and the economy moves to C. After the election the government wishes to deal with the high inflation at C, and so contracts the economy. The economy consequently moves to D, where there is stagflation. The arrows illustrate that inflation and unemployment are both higher at D than at A where we started.

Friedman also argued that Keynes was wrong about the slopes of the investment and money demand functions: his empirical research had shown that in fact the investment curve was relatively elastic (flat) and the money demand curve relatively inelastic (steep), the opposite of Keynes's claim (see Figure 5.4). This meant that fiscal policy was very ineffective in dealing with any macroeconomic problem because it caused a great deal of crowding out of interest-sensitive private expenditure (that is, a fiscal expansion would drive the interest rate up, say from R1 to R2, and so investment would fall,

Figure 5.4

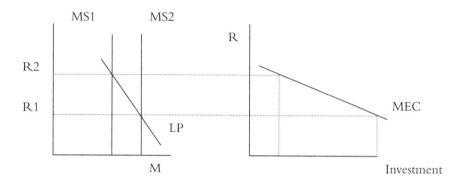

With a steep money demand curve (LP) and a very flat investment function (MEC), even a small change in the money supply (MS) will cause a large change in the interest rate (R) and thus a large change in investment and hence the size of the economy.

offsetting the fiscal expansion), but monetary policy was very effective, the reverse of what Keynes had argued.

Friedman advocated that during a period of stagflation the economy should be contracted using monetary policy: inflation, he argued, was a monetary phenomenon (too much money in the economy), thus reducing its supply was the solution. For Friedman, unemployment was not caused by insufficient aggregate demand, as it was for Keynes, but rather by labour markets failing to clear in an inflationary environment. There is an asymmetry between the perceptions or expectations of the employers and those of the employees. The former, with their esoteric knowledge (their knowledge of economic theory and of government policy) predict inflation correctly for the next time period, while the latter use the current inflation rate as their predictor. During a contractionary phase, inflation will fall, but employees, who lack the necessary knowledge, expect inflation to be the same in the next time period as in the present one. Consequently they expect that in the next time period inflation will be higher than it actually turns out to be and so they will not moderate their wage claims, which means that the nominal or money wage they are willing to work for will be higher than the one employers, who know inflation is falling, are willing to pay. As employers are not willing to pay enough in

Figure 5.5

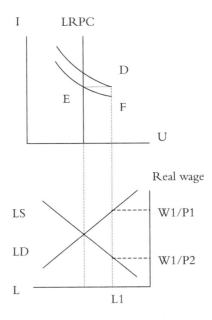

The upper part of the diagram above represents Friedman's long- and short-run Phillip's curves once again. The lower diagram is the labour market illustrated the *wrong way around*; this is because the X-axis measures the quantity of labour, or *employment*, whereas the X-axis of the top diagram measures *unemployment*. Thus making the X-axis of the lower diagram show *employment* as measured right to left means that it is illustrating the same thing as the X-axis of the top diagram, which shows *unemployment* left to right. The Y-axis of the lower diagram measures the real wage, viz. the nominal wage (W) divided by prices (P). We are examining the effects of a contractionary policy, so the economy is moving down the short-run Phillips curve to D (recall the journey we took in Figure 5.3), then on to E if inflation is held constant and to F if the government persists with its policy. As the economy is contracted the employers realise that inflation (or, for simplicity, prices) are falling (P1 rather than P2) and so want to offer a lower wage in the next time period, even if this does not quite compensate for the fall in inflation (W1 rather than W2, which was paid in the current time period), viz. a real wage of W1/P1, and given the labour demand curve LD, employers will demand L1 labour. Employees do not appreciate that inflation is falling, so they will assume that with a nominal wage offer of W1 that the real wage will be less (W1/P2) than it actually turns out to be in the next time period, and given the labour supply curve LS will also supply L1 labour. A quasi-equilibrium is thus established. If the government held inflation constant at D, employees would eventually realise that inflation was constant, they would moderate their wage demands, the labour market would clear and the economy would move to point E. As expected inflation is now lower, we are on a lower short-run Phillips curve. This important issue is taken up again in the next figure. But if the government persists with its policy to reduce inflation then the economy will move from E to F along the lower short-run Phillips curve for the same reason as we explained its movement to D along the higher short-run Phillips curve in the foregoing.

Figure 5.6

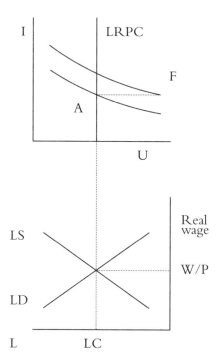

When inflation has fallen and is held constant by the government, the economy moves from point F to point A and the short-run Phillips curve moves down. As inflation is constant, both employers and employees will expect, in the next time period, the same inflation rate and so the employees will moderate their wage claims. This means that both employers and employees will demand and supply labour at the same real wage, the correct one. Thus at this real wage (W/P) the same amount of labour will be demanded and supplied respectively (LC) and so employment is determined where the labour demand and supply curves cross, and so the labour market clears and we have full employment.

employees' eyes, the employees supply less labour than is required for market clearing. Because employers know that inflation is falling and so the real wage (nominal or money wages divided by prices) is rising, they will demand less labour at the money wage for which employees are willing to work, which will be less labour than is needed for market clearing. So a quasi-equilibrium is arrived at where labour supply and demand are equated below market clearing (in other words, at less than full employment). Eventually, however, employees will realise that inflation is falling and moderate their wage claims accordingly. Once inflation is zero, or at least stable, both employers and employees predict or expect the correct inflation rate and therefore the correct real wage, labour is supplied and demanded at its correct market price, the labour market clears and we have full employment (see Figures 5.5 and 5.6). Furthermore, with the rise of index linked wage settlements, the asymmetry of expectations ceases to be relevant, so ensuring labour market clearance.

Margaret Thatcher employed policies based upon this theory, and unemployment rose to more than three million during the early 1980s, though this was largely due to the privatisation of state industries and the accelerated sectoral shift in the economy from being predominantly manufacturing to being comprised predominantly of service sector industries (see Chapter 11). Unemployment then fell gradually during the mid-to-late 1980s, though not below 1.5 million, which is approximately what it was when Thatcher came to power. Inflation, however, did fall successfully, though there was a brief rise in the late 1980s when Nigel Lawson was Chancellor of the Exchequer. When the stock markets crashed in 1987 there was a real fear of a global recession. Lawson employed expansionary monetary policy in consequence, but the major economies recovered more quickly than expected and so the monetary expansion proved excessive; leading to the 'Lawson boom'. This required a contraction in monetary policy, which together with the subsequent exchange rate policy (outlined below) caused a short lived-recession in the early 1990s, and unemployment rose again to 2.25 million by 1991.

Also, the monetary aggregates were not moving as the theory predicted. This was largely because Thatcher's laissez-faire deregulation of the financial services markets (see Chapter 9) enabled the private financial institutions to create money more readily (through loaning money and so creating new bank accounts for borrowers), and this made it more difficult for the Bank of England to control the money supply. Consequently the Treasury was obliged to introduce a narrow definition of money, known as 'M0', referring to notes and coins (and so not including bank deposits), and monetary policy was then intended to target this.

These policies were employed by the government of Thatcher's successor, John Major, and by New Labour's Tony Blair, who after eighteen years of Conservative rule adopted largely Conservative policies to get elected.

Thatcher also employed supply-side macroeconomic policies, namely improving economic efficiency by creating incentives to increase supply and so grow the economy in a disinflationary way. To this end, trade union activity was restricted, the government privatised nationalised industries (see Chapter 11), and the marginal rate of income tax was reduced from a maximum rate of 98% as it had been under Labour, to a top rate first of 60%

and then from 1988 of 40%. At the same time the marginal rate for basic rate tax payers was reduced to 27% and then in 1988 to 25%, and Norman Lamont when Chancellor of the Exchequer in the early 1990s introduced an additional introductory 10% band.

This last measure was promoted by the American economist Arthur Laffer, who argued that reducing the marginal rate of income tax increased the incentive for people to apply effort as they now kept an increased proportion of their own income. This increased effort would increase aggregate supply in the economy, which puts downward pressure on inflation and raises national output. Because the economy grows this means that the total tax yield to government grows, so everybody gains. This counter-intuitive notion that reducing the marginal rate of income tax causes total tax yield to rise is illustrated by the famous Laffer curve.

However, the effect that this reduction in income tax has on incentives has been debated. Subsequent research has tended to show that upper income groups do apply additional effort, and therefore increase output, but that lower income groups substitute leisure for work. Also it is argued that to some extent these policies stimulate the economy on the demand side rather than on the supply side, because by lowering income tax they increase disposable income and therefore private expenditure. This issue is taken up again in the next chapter.

The need to provide substantial unemployment benefits and other public expenditures meant that Thatcher could not reduce the tax burden overall without raising borrowing; as she believed in balancing the budget she would not do this. However, her first Chancellor of the Exchequer, Geoffrey Howe, altered the composition of the fiscal system, shifting the incidence from direct to indirect taxation. This change was done for ideological reasons as it represented a shift from collectivism to individualism.

When there is a high rate of income tax it is government which disposes national wealth through its expenditure programmes. When direct taxes are low, and disposable income is commensurately higher, it is the individual who disposes wealth. If the tax burden falls predominantly on the expenditure side, individuals can decide which taxes they pay by their expenditure choices, and people can avoid expenditure taxes by saving, and so increasing funds available for investment. However, at the end of Thatcher's eleven and a half years in office, despite the change in fiscal composition, the total tax take was still approximately the same as it had been when she had come to power; this represented a failure as she believed in a reduced role for government in resource allocation decisions, and it was clear that she had failed appreciably to reduce total government spending commitments.

The next Chancellor of the Exchequer, Nigel Lawson, was keen for Britain to enter the exchange rate mechanism (ERM) of the European Monetary System (EMS). He was in favour of further integration within the European Community, but Thatcher had been opposed to ERM entry as it meant that monetary policy could not be used exclusively to manage the domestic economy, and because she believed that free markets should determine economic values. However, in 1988 Lawson decided to use monetary policy to maintain a relatively constant exchange rate against the Deutschmark (DM). This inconsistency between Thatcher and Lawson was fuelled by the fact that Thatcher had employed the economist Alan Walters as her private advisor; he constantly railed against Lawson's policy, resulting in Lawson's resignation, and subsequently his own. Lawson was replaced as Chancellor by John Major, whom Thatcher had appointed only thirteen weeks earlier as Foreign Secretary. Thatcher felt obliged to do this because she wanted a Chancellor who would adopt her policies rather than his own, and she believed that Major would perform this function.

However, while Chancellor, Major was persuaded of the appropriateness of the fixed exchange rate policy and on 5 October 1990 he and the Cabinet persuaded Thatcher that Britain should join. Sterling entered the ERM at DM2.95 in the 6 per cent band within which it could fluctuate, with a ceiling of DM3.13 and floor of DM2.78. This was a comparatively high exchange rate at the time. This high rate was chosen because the government was convinced that it could both address the domestic inflation generated by the Lawson boom and use monetary policy to maintain the fixed exchange rate. The comparatively high exchange rate required a contractionary monetary policy to maintain it in order to attract capital from abroad and hence demand for sterling on the foreign exchange markets. This was disinflationary as it constrained domestic interest-sensitive expenditure. It was also disinflationary as it meant cheap import prices, and for a highly import-dependent economy such as Britain's, this was significant.

Major succeeded Thatcher as Prime Minister in November 1990, and the ERM became the central part of his macroeconomic policy. In January 1992 four out of five Conservative ministers approved of the policy, and sterling was trading at DM2.89, well within its band. Major won the general election in April 1992, but the problem came shortly thereafter when George Soros and other international investors decided that this exchange rate could not be justified by the economic fundamentals (the long-run productive efficiency of the economy) and started to sell sterling on the foreign exchange markets. The Bank of England was required to spend billions of foreign exchange reserves to defend the pound.

Major went to the German Chancellor, Helmut Kohl, and asked if the Bundesbank would buy sterling on the foreign exchange markets, a policy which it could theoretically undertake forever as it could simply print marks to buy sterling. This, the Major government assumed, would convey to the markets a determined policy to maintain sterling at the prescribed exchange rate. But Kohl was busy with reunifying the two Germanys and was not interested in British monetary difficulties. In early September 1992 Helmut Schlesinger, head of the Bundesbank, said he would not raise interest rates further to deal with internal German economic difficulties, a policy which had strengthened the mark at the expense of sterling, but promised no further help. Kohl told Major to devalue the pound, which the ERM permitted, but Major would not do this because of the adverse political consequences. Devaluing a currency is interpreted by the electorate as mismanagement of the economy and tends to be punished at elections, as had happened to Harold Wilson. Sterling approached its lower limit in the ERM on 16 September. The desire for a free market in the European Union meant that capital controls had been abandoned, so Soros and his colleagues could sell sterling easily.

The net cost of defending sterling amounted to £3.3bn while the total Bank of England expenditure was the largest in history at £28bn. In addition to this the Chancellor of the Exchequer, Norman Lamont, agreed that the Bank should raise interest rates massively, finally to an extraordinary 15 per cent, but the investment fund managers did not provide the capital flows necessary to keep the exchange rate within the 6 per cent band prescribed by the ERM. Consequently, on Wednesday 16 September 1992 Lamont announced that sterling was to be suspended from the ERM, a day which became known as Black Wednesday. George Soros made £1bn. However, this forced ejection from the system would lead to a reduction in both interest rates and the exchange rate, initiating a sustained period of economic growth which would last for more than a decade.

The Black Wednesday debacle contributed significantly to Major's general election defeat nearly five years later, as did Major's policy of raising taxation massively to finance increased public expenditure, having campaigned in the 1992 general election that only a Labour government if elected would do that.

The first significant act of Tony Blair's New Labour government was for the Chancellor of the Exchequer, Gordon Brown, to create an independent Monetary Policy Committee (MPC) in the Bank of England, made up of bankers and academics, to determine monetary policy. Prior to this governments were directly responsible for monetary policy, as they were for fiscal policy. This change was undertaken because Labour governments had developed a reputation for poor economic management by comparison with Conservative ones, and this act removed the principal instrument of macroeconomic policy from government control. However, the Chancellor of the Exchequer retains control over the inflation target which the MPC is obliged to hit, and the Chancellor is also responsible for the appointment of part of the MPC; this gives the government overall control of monetary policy.

The Blair government stuck to the Conservative expenditure plans for their first two years, but then embarked on a policy of raising indirect taxes substantially to fund their public service plans, thereby initiating the so-called stealth taxes. If the marginal rate of income tax is raised, we all blame the government; if expenditure taxes are raised, we blame the shops! So stealth taxes were principally the subtle raising of indirect taxation, though personal allowances were not indexed properly with inflation and so direct tax also rose.

The Chancellor also introduced his 'golden rule' that government spending – excluding capital expenditures – must be in balance or in surplus across the economic cycle. This is his notion of fiscal prudence. However, the extent to which the golden rule is met is determined by the ambiguity between the definitions of current expenditure and investment or capital spending, whether the balance is measured in absolute terms or as a proportion of GDP in a fiscal year, and the length of the economic cycle. In July 2005 the economic cycle was extended by the Chancellor from seven to nine years, enabling the budget surpluses of 1997 and 1998 to facilitate additional current borrowing without violating the golden rule.

The overall result of the Labour governments' policies has been to ensure sustained low inflation; but unemployment, contrary to popular belief, has remained high at around 1.5 million. This figure is as measured by the International Labour Organisation, the preferred Labour government measure. The Thatcher government had altered the way unemployment was measured, principally by measuring only those claiming unemployment benefit (to give the impression unemployment was less than it actually was). This official measure was retained by the Blair government, and when measured this way unemployment is about 1 million, still historically high. The composition of the workforce has changed in the last few years, with some loss of jobs in the private sector but growth in employment in the public sector.

Regarding the European single currency, the euro, the official government position is that Britain is in favour of joining if the economic conditions are conducive to the national interest. To this end Brown, who, unlike Blair, is not a supporter of euro membership (along with others in the party), proposed five economic tests that must be met if Britain were to join. These tests have shifted the decision for entry to the Treasury and were intended to constitute an impediment to adopting the euro. They are:

1. Sustainable convergence between the British economy and that of the existing euro zone economies.
2. Sufficient flexibility to address economic change.
3. The effect of the euro on investment.
4. The effect of the euro on the financial services industry.
5. Whether the euro is good for employment.

No quantitative thresholds have been provided, thus it is a political judgement rather than an economic one as to whether these tests have been passed or not.

Blair promised the electorate a referendum prior to joining; as opinion polls consistently show a majority of the British electorate opposed, the referendum and hence euro entry have been postponed indefinitely.

Conclusion

Britain was virtually bankrupt in 1945, and its rate of economic recovery was relatively slow. This was not the result of poor macroeconomic policy per se, though Milton Friedman would argue that the policies which were used created the stagflation suffered by the industrial economies in the late 1960s and 1970s. Rather, the problem was really one of productivity, or the lack of it, and this is determined by education, training and technology rather than by macroeconomic policy. Notwithstanding, macroeconomic management up until 1979 was marked by policy reversals, which did nothing to enhance economic performance.

Between 1993 and 2004 (approximately) Britain enjoyed its best macroeconomic record in modern times. Gross domestic product (GDP) for 2004 was $2.12 trillion, and the economy grew by 3.1 per cent in that year. British economic growth has been higher than that of the rest of the EU, averaging a growth rate of 2.6 per cent per annum in the early twenty-first century, as opposed to 2.0 per cent per annum for the EU as a whole. This contrasts sharply with the post-war period, when Britain's economy lurched from one crisis to the next. But the change in macroeconomic policy was only partly responsible for this; it was the sectoral shift in the structure of the economy, from one based on manufacturing and the extractive industries with poor productivity to a more highly productive service-sector based economy, which was responsible for the transformation, and we set this out in detail in Chapter 11. However, the proportion of GDP taken in tax by the government has risen from 39 per cent in 1979 to 42.5 per cent in 2005, greater than in almost every major industrial nation, and the cumulative effect of this caused economic growth to fall to 1.7 per cent in 2005. Also, if we consider all of the 'economically inactive', namely those in society who do not have a job, whether they are categorised officially as unemployed or not, and including those who took early retirement, then the total figure is almost eight million!

6

Social security and pensions policies

Introduction

The welfare state in Britain is very comprehensive in its structure. It has been subject to detailed changes but not fundamental reform since it was created immediately after the Second World War, though its foundations had been laid before the First World War. Covering pensions, unemployment and sickness payments, it offers state-financed benefits of a wide and complex nature. All governments have kept it largely intact, and it remains the cornerstone of policy today.

The welfare state is a notion which came into common parlance in the years immediately after the Second World War. A blueprint was developed by William Beveridge, a Liberal politician and a member of the war-time coalition government. He was asked to develop policies to address post-war social issues, and the report he produced advocated providing state social protection for the public 'from cradle to grave'. The report, which was published in 1942, formed the basis of the post-war consensus on the welfare state, though, as with most of these consensus policies, the Conservatives were initially opposed – on ideological grounds as well as cost.

It had been the reforming Liberal government of Herbert Asquith (1908–1916) which introduced state pensions in 1908 and selective compulsory sickness and unemployment benefits in 1911. But in the inter-war period there had been limited social provision, and great hardship was endured by a substantial proportion of the populace during the Depression of the 1930s. The Second World War brought full employment, but rationing restricted the consumption of many household goods, and there was the obvious physical damage, injury and death caused by the conflict.

The electorate's shift to the left by 1945 and its desire to ensure a level of social provision which would end the hardship and restrictions of the 1930s and early 1940s ushered in a Labour government. It thus had a mandate to transform social provision in Britain, and so the welfare state was introduced, and became part of the post-war consensus, and in modified form remains with us today.

The 1945 Labour manifesto, 'Let Us Face the Future', pledged a Labour government to eliminating the 'five evil giants of want, squalor, disease, ignorance and unemployment'. The government implemented the Beveridge report and this led to the 1946 National Insurance Act, which largely brought the existing benefits laid down by the pre-First World War Liberal government under a single system. As with Asquith's Liberal policies, the link between benefit entitlement and payment was retained, so a system of national insurance contributions (NICs) was initiated to facilitate this. Under the 1946 Act those of working age were obliged to purchase a weekly stamp, the cost of which was determined by age, gender, marital status and employment. Employers were also required to make a contribution to this entitlement. The benefit entitlements were for unemployment, maternity, sickness, widowhood and pension, and a death grant was provided to pay for funeral costs. The National Insurance (Industrial Injuries) Act of the same year introduced additional benefits for those who sustained injuries at work. The Beveridge report had assumed that a contributory period of about twenty years would be necessary to provide for a full pension entitlement; however, the Labour government decided to introduce such an entitlement from October 1946, the retirement age for men being sixty-five and for women sixty.

The National Assistance Act of 1948 introduced the modern 'safety net' system, as it provided benefits for those not covered by the 1946 Acts. Prior to the Second World War there had been a body called the Assistance Board, responsible for providing benefits, which after the war evolved into the National Assistance Board and became responsible for administering means-tested benefits for those not in full-time employment and who lacked a subsistence income. This board was eventually abolished in 1966 and replaced by the Supplementary Benefits Commission with wider-ranging responsibilities. The post-war legislation also introduced a system of family support which had two components: firstly, a taxable family allowance for the second and all subsequent children of each family; and secondly, an income tax allowance for every child of each family. However, this proved to be a complicated system which did not ensure that benefits went to the most in need.

The NICs which people were obliged to make to this system were flat rate, which meant that they were highly regressive, as they constituted a higher proportion of the wages of the low paid than those of the higher paid. Also, as the flat rate contributions had to be affordable for the poorest, this meant that the total contributions, and so total funds yielded by the system, were only sufficient to provide a very basic system of provision. The system was consequently changed so that by the 1960s, NICs became a percentage of income, not a flat rate, and provision of benefit was to be financed out of the general tax pool and not simply from the NICs themselves. Also, NICs are not hypothecated to the benefit system but have become an additional tranche of income tax. These changes financed substantially increased welfare provision, but eliminated the notion that people's entitlement should be predicated on their payment into the system. The new purpose of making NICs was merely to give entitlement to be in receipt of benefits. In 1965 the earnings-related supplement (ERS) of unemployment and sickness benefits was introduced, which augmented these benefits with a supplementary payment positively correlated with earnings.

The total social security budget (including pensions) constitutes nearly half of the entire government budget. This was administered by the Department of Health and Social Security until the Thatcher era, when the responsibilities of state health care provision were separated off into the Department of Health, while social security was administered on its own by the Department of Social Security. By the twenty-first century social security benefits would be administered by the Department for Work and Pensions.

In the 1970s, research had shown that the social security system had only marginally reduced income inequality and that poverty remained endemic. This was partly due to the fact that the middle classes enjoyed financial concessions within the fiscal system; for example, home owners received tax relief on mortgage interest repayments (see Chapter 9) and contributions towards private or occupational pensions were also subject to tax relief.

In 1971 Edward Heath's Conservative government introduced a family income supplement. This was a benefit intended for working adults with dependent children. However, to receive it, people had to apply formally for it, and so a problem was incurred which is common with such benefits, namely that there was a poor take up rate, as many eligible people were unaware of their eligibility and so didn't apply. Also it illustrated another basic problem with the system, that of 'churning', where people are in receipt of benefits and subject to tax simultaneously. For example, certain families were eligible for family income supplement but also simultaneously subject to income tax, so what is given with one hand is taken away with the other.

The Labour government of Harold Wilson introduced the Social Security Pensions Act of 1975 which both created statutory earnings-related pensions and introduced the indexation of pensions so they would rise as average earnings rose. This was to have a redistributive effect from rich to poor. The government also introduced the Child Benefit Act in the same year, abolishing two elements of the post-war legislation: the family allowance and the child tax allowance. The Act introduced a weekly tax-free child benefit for every child in each family, and also introduced an additional tranche for single parents.

In the 1975 Social Security Act the Labour government introduced a flat-rate weekly pension, which was one-fifth of the average earnings of a single person. The Act also introduced an earnings-related component, the State Earnings-Related Pension Scheme (SERPS). The latter was calculated on the basis of the highest earning twenty years from a person's working life. A married man was to receive a pension of higher value than a single man, unless his wife was also in receipt of a pension. For those who worked beyond retirement age, the pension was increased by an amount for each additional year worked. Entitlement required contributions for twenty years subsequent to the introduction of the scheme, or forty-four years for men and forty for women from the old 1948 scheme.

With unemployment growing significantly by the mid-1970s the Wilson government also introduced community development projects to deal with social deprivation. Subsequently the Callaghan government introduced the Job Creation Programme, a government-subsidised system whereby organisations would be paid government funds to create employment directly. This was anathema to Margaret Thatcher, who would scrap this system, introduce training schemes for the unemployed and offer a reduced benefit rate to those undertaking voluntary work. This was much more consistent with her belief in supply side reforms, whereby the government acts as a facilitator to provide opportunity, but the market mechanism is used to create jobs, not the government.

The Thatcher government was unable to radically reform the social security budget as unemployment rose dramatically in the 1980s and so demands on social security provision rose as a consequence. It did, however, make a few structural changes: in 1982 it scrapped the 1965 ERS for unemployment and sickness benefits, returning to a flat-rate system. Also, instead of benefit and pension increases being indexed to the rate at which average earnings were rising, they were indexed to inflation. As prices were rising more slowly than earnings this reduced government expenditure on these benefits, but at the expense of slowly increasing income inequality between those employed and those on benefit. Indeed, during the Thatcher period of government the rich would get richer and the poor would become poorer generally. Real per capita income in Britain rose by 36 per cent during this period, but the poorest 10 per cent were nearly 13 per cent worse off in absolute terms, while the richest 10 per cent grew 60 per cent better off.

In the twenty years after the Second World War, the total number of people receiving benefits had almost doubled, and this prompted some heretical thinking about the system in the late 1970s. Statistical evidence showed that the ratio of unemployment benefits received by married couples with two children to average net earnings, and the level of unemployment, had both risen substantially. This would indicate that generous unemployment benefits created a disincentive to work and thus the average duration of unemployment had risen. However, some theorists argue that this empirical evidence is not robust. One reason for this is that employment is often preferred to unemployment, thus psychological reasons militate to reduce or eliminate the disincentive effect of generous benefit levels. Nevertheless the New Right political theorists promoted neo-liberal free-market ideas and the notion of incentives to work (low taxation) and disincentives to remain idle (less generous social security benefits).

The Thatcher government decided to reduce the marginal rates of income tax (see Chapter 5) to improve welfare and efficiency. However, the empirical evidence regarding the extent to which changes in the tax system are causally effective in increasing the amount of employment amongst low-income groups is inconclusive. There are studies which demonstrate that reductions in the tax burden to the lower paid enhance welfare and reduce poverty. It is often argued that the labour supply curve slopes first backwards then forwards, because an increase in the net wage, in this case resulting from a fall in the marginal rate of income tax, reduces hours worked for low-income workers but increases effort and so hours worked by the higher paid. This means that the low paid will substitute leisure for work as their disposable income rises, but the high paid are more incentivised to work when they can keep a higher proportion of their incomes. The upshot of this is that if only small reductions in the marginal rate of income tax are provided to the lowest paid, then there could in fact be a fall in the amount of work done! Therefore, the tax incentives must apply to the higher-income earners, up the forward-bending part of the curve, if the policy is to be effective in raising effort and so economic output. It must be stressed that the empirical evidence suggests that the increase in work effort resulting from such tax changes is small. However, the tax reductions may certainly be justified on grounds of social justice, that is by enhancing social welfare amongst the lowest paid.

The Thatcher government changed the whole basis of the social security system: no longer would the welfare state encompass everybody, but it would only provide a safety net for those in need. People were encouraged to opt out of SERPS and start a private pension scheme. However, a problem arose because private financial services companies became responsible for misselling personal pensions (endowments) during the 1980s. Also, the publisher of Mirror Group Newspapers, Robert Maxwell, stole hundreds of millions in the early 1990s from the company pension fund to finance the business when it faced serious trouble. As a result the government introduced the Occupational Pensions Regulator to regulate company pensions schemes. More recently, final-salary pensions schemes, where pensions are based on the last salary paid, which tends to be the highest in a person's career, have become very expensive to fund and are increasingly being closed.

John Major's Conservative government introduced the jobseekers' allowance in 1996, paying a flat rate benefit for those single people who are actively seeking work and are aged at least twenty-five. The jobseekers' allowance replaced unemployment benefit and was to be paid either on the basis of the recipient having a record of making NICs (in which case it was paid for six months like the old unemployment benefit), or on a means-tested basis. This was significant, because the nomenclature indicated that benefit was now for those actively seeking work, and the basis of payment was no longer determined only by a contributions record. Also, statutory sick pay was to replace sickness benefit, which had been introduced immediately after the war. The new benefit would be administered by employers and would be taxable, and its receipt would be dependent upon a record of contributions. Statutory maternity pay was introduced on the same basis, as was incapacity benefit, which is for long-term sickness. Severe disablement allowance, a tax-free benefit, was introduced for those not entitled to incapacity benefit because they lacked a contributions record.

The most important single issue of the post-war benefit system has been the 'poverty trap'; this is where people in receipt of benefits whose incomes rise through obtaining a job or enjoying a pay rise or working overtime are subject to a withdrawal of benefits. This can leave them little better off or sometimes worse off, meaning that there is a disincentive to work, and it becomes almost impossible to increase the family income. This could be addressed by withdrawing benefits at a much reduced rate as incomes rise; however, the additional cost to the Exchequer of so doing would require either a much higher incidence of tax on middle income groups, or lower levels of benefit for the poor. So the pretext for the poverty trap is the attempt to protect middle income groups from penal rates of taxation and yet to provide reasonable benefits to the poor.

As we have seen, many benefits are means tested; that is, their receipt is contingent upon meeting certain criteria, an example of this being disability benefit. Other benefits are universal irrespective of a person's income, such as child benefit. The latter tend to be inefficient as much of the benefit is received by families who have middle incomes or higher and thus do not need it. In the case of child benefit, government calculations showed that almost half was received by families with above-average incomes. This was used to justify the freezing of the benefit. Thus, the principal argument for additional means testing is that there are financial and welfare gains of so doing. Switching from universal benefits to means-tested ones results in a redistribution of income from the richest to the poorest section of the population, with the poorest section gaining the most. Thus means testing targets benefits more effectively for the poor. However, as mentioned earlier, the withdrawal of benefits as incomes rise is the cause of the poverty trap: the more benefits which are means tested, the greater the poverty trap. Also, means-tested benefits cost more to administer than universal benefits, in some cases nearly ten times more!

The unemployed, sick, disabled or retired are more likely to be subject to low incomes than are other groups in society, the National Insurance system as presently structured pays benefits to those groups for precisely that reason.

New Labour introduced the notions of communitarianism and the stakeholder into social policy determination. The former refers to the notion that people should have some sense of social obligation in return for receiving welfare benefits, and the latter that people should have some clearly perceived vested interest or stake in society, for only if this is so would they have any motivation to contribute to society rather than simply take what they could from it. The net result was an acceptance of the New Right shift from the 'equality of outcome' of the old post-war consensus to 'equality of opportunity', that inequalities were justified if they were the consequence of people's effort (or the lack of it). Also, there was the acceptance by New Labour of private sector solutions to the provision of public services.

To this end, the indexing of welfare payments to inflation rather than to average earnings was retained by New Labour (though pensions are to be linked again to earnings by 2012); however, mortgage interest tax relief was reduced and eventually eliminated (see Chapter 9) and the tax advantages which applied to private pensions were scrapped. This resulted in an additional £5 billion per annum being transferred from private pensions to the Treasury in tax revenue. Also, because of the scandal of missold private pensions in the 1980s, the government regulator of the private pension system now requires that private pension schemes acquire safe investments, which are thus low yielding. In consequence pension funds may have difficulty in the future in fulfilling their obligations for pensions provision.

The issue of social exclusion (addressed by a stakeholder society) was dealt with by the creation of the Social Exclusion Unit, which was located in the Cabinet Office in Downing Street and was responsible directly to the Prime Minister. Its function was primarily to coordinate the activities of the various government departments responsible for social policy issues, but it was provided with a budget of just £1 million and a staff of no more than a dozen and so was necessarily limited in its influence.

The jobseekers' allowance remained under New Labour; although this benefit was introduced by the previous Conservative government, it is entirely consistent with the New Labour stakeholder notion, for an interview must indicate that the person intends actively to seek work. A job seekers' agreement has to be signed by those in reciept of such benefits, which commits the person actively to seek a specified type of employment, with the assistance of the Employment Service.

In order to increase the effectiveness of this policy, New Labour introduced the New Deal. This involved a new scheme called 'welfare to work' which followed American and Australian models, and was intended to encourage people to reduce their reliance on benefits and to gain employment. In consequence, under the jobseekers' allowance scheme, people between the ages of eighteen and twenty-four who have been claiming benefit for six months are obliged to accept a job subsidised by government, enrol on a training course or accept employment in a voluntary organisation, or else have their benefit cut. The results of this scheme are poor, with many accepting reduced benefits and continuing to be unemployed. The original American scheme upon which it is based, Workfare, has been much more successful than the British scheme as all benefits are removed with non-compliance. The British government has not been prepared to go this far.

On the same theme, to encourage those single parents and the disabled in receipt of benefits to gain employment, such people were obliged to receive advice on employment or training from government advisors. But as there was no penalty for non-compliance few bothered. Even though attendance for single parents was made compulsory the results of the policy remain mixed.

New Labour has also introduced a series of benefits called tax credits. In economics parlance this notion refers to a reduction in liability to income tax, but New Labour have used this term to refer to a cash benefit to be received by eligible people, whether they are paying income tax or not earning at all! The reason for this is largely propaganda – it is to convey a sense that it isn't really a benefit at all, but simply a tax allowance, when it is nothing of the kind. There are two of these tax credits. Firstly, the child tax credit is for those responsible (parent or not) for one or more children. The value is determined by the number of children, whether a child is disabled, and by the person's income. Secondly, there is the working tax credit, for those in employment but receiving low pay. Additional benefit is available if the person is responsible for a child, has to pay for child care, lives in a household with at least one disabled member, or is over fifty.

Currently the state pension entitlement is determined by the the number of qualifying years each person has paid NICs. With greater life expectancy and fewer children being born to each family the proportion of the population in receipt of pensions continues to grow. By 2050 the proportion of the population aged over sixty is expected to rise from 21.2 per cent, as it is now, to 29.4 per cent. At the beginning of the twenty-first century a 65-year-old man can expect to live to 86 years and 10 months, but by 2015 this is estimated to rise to 89 years and 10 months. Female life expectancy is due to exceed 90, but the traditional gender gap is narrowing. These changes are due to higher real per capita incomes, improved diets and medical advances. Given that no part of the NICs are hypothecated to pension provision, and thus all state pensions are funded out of the current general tax pool, this means that it is currently those members of the younger generation who are in work who are burdened with the greatest share of financing these pension payments. As this demographic portion of society diminishes so the cost burden per person rises. This creates a long-run pension 'time bomb', which governments are reluctant to tackle as it means either higher pension contributions, lower pensions, a higher retirement age or a combination of all three. These are unpopular options and, as any government has a limited time horizon (the next election), governments tend to emphasise short-run policies to attract electoral support at the expense of long-run policies to address deep-seated issues.

However, the Blair government has decided that the age of pension entitlement for women should be raised to that of men (sixty-five) by 2020. Related to this, the Pensions Commission published the Turner report on 30 November 2005. This report suggested that further measures were required. It recommended that the age of pension entitlement should rise to sixty-six by 2030, then to sixty-seven by 2040 and sixty-eight by 2050. The government decided to enact each of these changes six years early. The report also recommended the introduction of a new National Pension Savings Scheme (NPSS) by 2010. The purpose of this scheme would be to act as social insurance for those without secure private pensions, and for those not eligible for a pension scheme at all. Those not currently enrolled in a workplace pension scheme would be automatically enrolled into the NPSS, and employers would be required to make contributions. Employees would have the facility to opt out of the scheme if they could make other satisfactory pension arrangements, and employers could also opt out if they offered their own pension scheme with at least equal terms to that of the NPSS. The government decided to introduce such a system in 2012. The report also recommended that, as the pension age is to be increased under the proposals, the government introduce age discrimination legislation in order to ensure that people continue to be employable right up to the higher retirement age, and that government training schemes should offer provision for the older workers as well as the young.

Conclusion

Social security remains the largest single expenditure item undertaken by government, dwarfing that of virtually all other spending departments. There is no doubt that it offers social protection for (virtually) all in society, but the question remains as to what effect this vast expenditure on benefits has on incentives to work and on unemployment. The attempts by Margaret Thatcher to reduce its scope amounted to little, for expenditure on social security continued to grow, and although the New Labour government has extended the Conservative reforms, they are not having any significant effect as yet. But as the Labour government is also committed to addressing poverty through redistribution, the social security budget remains on an upward trend.

7

Health service policies

Introduction

The National Health Service (NHS) is a unique institution providing health care cover to all British subjects, and is the most significant single element of the welfare state. Never before did Britain have such a publicly funded system of health care provision. There remains a private health care sector, which has grown in recent years, but the bulk of health care services continue to be delivered through the NHS. Its structure was reformed fundamentally to improve efficiency in the 1980s and again at the beginning of the twenty-first century, but the basic system remains the most cherished of the post-war welfare state policies amongst the British people.

The Secretary of State for Health in Clement Attlee's Labour government, Aneurin Bevan, was charged with setting up the NHS, and the National Health Service Act of 1946 led to the inauguration of the new service in 1948. Under the NHS, health care services were provided by the state and paid for out of taxation, the services being free at the point of delivery.

Initially Bevan had wanted doctors to be employed by the NHS, but their resistance to becoming part of the state system left them effectively self-employed but contracted to the NHS. Bevan had also wanted prescriptions to be free, but to keep costs down the government decided that prescriptions were to be subject to a charge for most patients. Bevan also had to accept the provision of some private beds (for fee-paying patients) in NHS hospitals. Dentistry and opticians' services, though subsidised under the NHS, were also not provided free to all at the point of delivery for the same reason.

The basic structure of the NHS was as follows: the country was divided up into a series of administrative areas, and government bureaucracies were set up in these areas to administer (at local level) the provision of NHS services. These were known as district health authorities (DHAs). NHS hospitals in the region of each DHA were directly administered by that authority, funding being provided by central government under the Resource Allocation Working Party (RAWP) formula, that is, on the basis of population size and local need. For example, a DHA with a disproportionately large geriatric population would require additional resources. Primary health care was provided by family practitioner committees, groups of general practitioners (GPs) in local practices who would liaise with hospitals and DHAs, funding being provided again by central government. GPs are doctors with general medical skills, but no speciality, who act as the first interface between the public and the health system.

This was a unique service which guaranteed equality of access to all patients irrespective of income and wealth and has constituted the central and most endearing legacy of the Attlee government.

Bevan assumed that there was a considerable backlog of medical disorders which required treatment, and that these disorders had not been treated successfully under the pre-war system, which was largely private with a means-tested public sector, as many were denied access to these services. The NHS was to undertake this task and thus rapidly improve the health of the overall population. This would lead to a fall in the total cost of health service provision as the process was accomplished. To some extent, with immunisation programmes for example, some disorders were (virtually) eliminated, but the development of medical technology enabled the effective treatment of many disorders which could not be treated before. This had two effects: the chronically ill could now be kept alive longer at great and increasing expense to the health service, and the greater life expectancy (which was being caused by other factors such as growing real per capita incomes as well as improving medical technology) meant that a higher proportion of the population was geriatric and thus increasingly subject to geriatric complaints. This meant that far from there being an overall fall in the costs of health care provision, the total costs persistently increased.

However, by comparison with other major industrial countries, Britain was spending less as a proportion of GDP on its health service provision. This was largely a consequence of the fact that expenditure on the NHS was part of total government expenditure and was therefore subject to the same cost constraints as were other government spending departments. This had implications for health outcomes, and the most significant of these was the fact that life expectancy in Britain remained lower than in many other industrial nations.

The basic problem with a system such as the NHS is that, whereas in a free

market, the price and output solution equilibrates at the intersection of a
downward-sloping demand curve and an upward-sloping supply curve, with
the NHS this does not happen, as output pricing is set at zero. When the price
is zero the demand for health care services is where the demand curve
intercepts the X-axis (illustrated as D(u) in Figure 7.1), this point is known as
'unconstrained demand'. To equilibrate the market, supply (which is perfectly
inelastic, as price does not influence supply conditions) would have to be set
at the point of unconstrained demand (S(u)).

The decision as to where to place the supply curve is a political one. It is a
matter for government to decide the total national tax take, national
borrowing and the proportion of total expenditure devoted to each spending
department, including health service provision. Health service expenditure

Figure 7.1

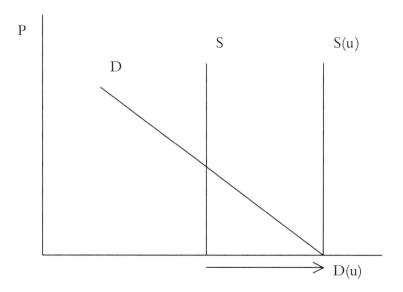

Price (P) is represented on the Y-axis, quantity of health care services on the X-axis. For the
NHS, where services are free at the point of delivery (price is zero), demand (D) will be where
the demand curve intercepts the X-axis, viz. unconstrained demand, illustrated by D(u). If this
is satisfied by supply S(u), viz unconstrained supply, then supply and demand are in equilibrium
at zero price. If, because of political constraints, supply is less than this (S), then there is excess
demand over supply equal to the length of the arrow on the X-axis.

now becomes part of macroeconomic policy. Thus in times of economic constraint, which occurred many times in the post-war years, total government expenditure, including health service expenditure, had to be restricted. But unconstrained demand would require such high government expenditure on health service provision that even during more benign periods it is almost impossible for any government to achieve. As a consequence the supply curve for health services was persistently located to the left of the point of unconstrained demand (S in Figure 7.1).

The notion of unconstrained demand assumes that the demand curve intercepts the X-axis. However, it is possible that the aggregate demand curve will asymptote (approach but never reach the X-axis; see Figure 7.2). This may happen if we broaden health service provision to include the treatment of relatively trivial matters such as cosmetic surgery, as well as life-threatening conditions, meaning that with output pricing set at zero, the market can never equilibrate.

Figure 7.2

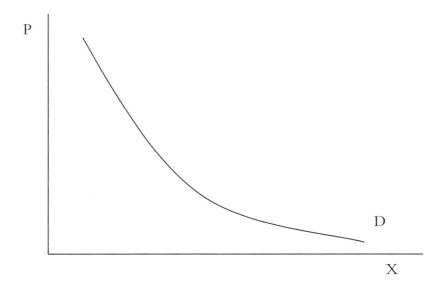

Here the demand curve asymptotes; that is, it approaches but never reaches the X-axis. Now, whether the supply curve is constrained or not, there will always be infinite excess demand over supply as price is set at zero.

Whether the demand curve asymptotes or hits the X-axis, the fact that supply is constrained for political reasons results in a situation of excess demand over supply, which is illustrated by the horizontal arrow in Figure 7.1, when the demand curve hits the X-axis. If demand asymptotes then the excess demand will be infinite. The only solution to this situation is rationing.

This rationing is manifest in waiting lists for elective operations and other forms of treatment. In 2002 some 22.1 per cent of patients were waiting between six and twelve months for treatment, and 3.2 per cent remained untreated after twelve months. There was no formal acceptance of this problem and so it was, by default, left to clinicians and administrators to take responsibility for this process. They would attempt to prioritise cases on the basis of clinical need.

In the limiting case rationing risks distressing consequences. Elderly, infirm patients when in hospital may be subject to the clinical decision 'do not resuscitate'. This is legitimately justified on clinical grounds, for such patients may not withstand defibrillation if in cardiac arrest. However, it also represents a value judgement concerning the allocation of health care resources. A less distressing but nevertheless problematic issue can be found in doctors' waiting rooms: as there is no charge to see a GP, waiting rooms contain among their patients some with the most trivial complaints, displacing GP time from attending to more important ones. Despite these problems, the notion of free access to health care has remained the most enduringly popular of government policies. All subsequent governments have been obliged to retain it.

In 1990 the Thatcher government introduced reforms to the health service. Margaret Thatcher realised that privatising the NHS would be very unpopular as it would eliminate free treatment to anyone who needed it. In consequence making the NHS more efficient would require retaining the basic overall structure: services free at the point of delivery which were financed out of the general tax pool. However, her government wanted to introduce commercial disciplines, and so created quasi- or provider markets within the NHS.

To create a market structure in the NHS it was necessary to separate the functions of supply and demand and to create competition in the supply of health care services. This policy worked in the following way: originally the district health authorities were responsible for both the provision and the purchase of health services, as to some extent were the general practices. Instead, the DHAs would now purchase health care services on behalf of the public (with taxpayers' money) and the NHS hospitals would compete to provide them at the lowest cost. Each DHA, being the sole organisation demanding health care services from NHS hospitals in each region (this is known as a monopsony), enabled the DHAs to drive down costs further. Just as a monopoly, a single supplier, drives prices up, so the power of a single demander for health services drives prices down.

Under the reforms NHS hospitals were offered the opportunity of acquiring 'trust status', in other words being self-governing like commercial businesses with a high degree of autonomy, though the assets remained state owned. Trust status was to be applied for voluntarily by the larger hospitals; it was not compulsory, for it was expected that trust status hospitals would outperform those which remained directly managed in competing for DHA contracts for services. Thus all major hospitals would eventually see the benefit of becoming trusts.

The equivalent status for general practices was that of fundholder, a self-governing practice where the GPs were given a high degree of autonomy in running it. Funded by the taxpayer, fundholder practices could increase the supply of services in house where this was possible (for minor treatments only), rather than commissioning all such services from hospitals if they felt they could make savings by so doing; any savings they made could be invested in the practice or used to increase salaries. Again this was voluntary because fundholders were expected to perform better than non-fundholders and so eventually all GPs would see the benefit of converting.

Empirical evidence is ambiguous regarding the efficiency gains of this system, largely because the former structure of the NHS proved effective at cost containment because of government budgetary constraints. In health care provision we do not have an adequate production function (relationship between inputs – doctors, nurses, equipment – and outputs – healthy patients), which means that it is difficult to apply the sort of cost–benefit analysis which would be found in the provision of most traded goods and services, and this impacts on efficiency. To the extent that we do know the relationship, the inputs tend to be non-substitutable, so as staff salaries rise over time (which they have) it is not possible to move to a more efficient capital-intensive system of health care provision. Indeed, to the extent that more capital is provided, it is because of advances in medical technology which have resulted in new equipment, at increasing cost.

Another problem with measuring the efficiency of the provision of health care services is the natural recuperative powers of the body. When I take my car into a garage for repair, the mechanic is entirely responsible for the rectification of the fault; but when I go to my GP with an ailment, and he or she gives me a prescription for some medicine, to what extent is the medicine responsible for my recovery and to what extent would I have recovered anyway? This problem makes it very difficult to measure the efficacy of many medical treatments.

As the result of these problems, a discipline of 'health economics' has developed in recent years to undertake research into the efficiency of health care provision. Health economists attempt to analyse the improvement in the quality of a patient's life as the result of specific medical treatments (itself a very difficult thing to measure), compare this with other treatments and so prioritise those treatments. So, for example, artificial hip replacements are relatively low cost, have a high rate of success, and considerably improve the quality of life of patients, so these might be prioritised over, say, heart transplants, which are very expensive, have a lower rate of success, and offer limited extension to life expectancy.

The New Labour government of Tony Blair, having initially expressed opposition to the introduction of quasi-markets, and instead emphasised cooperation between the elements of the health service, then proceeded to extend the implementation of quasi-markets. Having first committed them-selves to the former Conservative government's spending plans for its first two years in power, Labour then, in a health plan introduced in 2000, raised spending on the NHS by half in five years in nominal terms and by a third in real terms. The NHS was to be decentralised further while the Department of Health determined national standards and monitored the system. A new organisation called the National Institute for Clinical Excellence (NICE) was set up to license cost-effective drugs for the system, along with new bodies called 'care trusts', intended to commission health and social care collectively in one organisation. To make the system more flexible, nurses and other health staff were given the authority to administer drugs. In order to increase competition in the supply of hospital services and provide more capacity, a concordat was established whereby private hospitals could provide health services to the NHS. In 2002 the DHAs were replaced with new strategic health authorities and primary care trusts were introduced with decentralised powers, replacing both the fundholding and non-fundholding general practices.

A new type of hospital was introduced by the New Labour government, the foundation hospital. Foundation hospitals own and control former NHS assets. They are licensed by the government to operate and are overseen by an independent regulator; they are accountable not to the Secretary of State for

Health, but rather to a stakeholder board comprising employers, staff and local residents (some locally elected). These boards govern each hospital on a not-for-profit basis. The local residents are intended to provide local accountability; however, it is difficult to see how they will influence the health care professionals and senior hospital managers with their esoteric knowledge. As part of the decentralisation process, foundation hospitals enjoy greater freedom to determine their terms and conditions of employment, they may sell land associated with the hospital and retain the proceeds, they may raise finance from the capital markets subject to government borrowing limits, and they are able to set up joint ventures with the private sector. However, they may not sell off their core assets. All hospitals are to have foundation status by 2007. These hospitals are very much Blair's creation and are opposed by the left in his party.

The principal difference between the new system and Margaret Thatcher's is that patient choice is intended to drive the system, rather than competition between providers driving down prices. To this end, patients have been able to choose both the provider and the individual clinical team since 2005. Money is provided on the basis of patients treated, 'money following the patient'. However, it would seem that these changes must affect competition on the supply side, despite government protestation to the contrary. Also, providers will have a strong incentive not to offer treatment to chronically ill patients and so select the patients they do treat on the basis of minimising hospital stay.

In 2005 hospital statistics such as death rates were published, along with GP performance league tables. These tables are to provide patients with information to enable them to make judgements regarding the best hospital or GP to seek treatment from. This information is essential for consumer sovereignty, as service demand is increasingly influenced by patients rather than by clinicians, as was the case with the old NHS. This is a necessary condition for quasi-markets to function, and also a clear indication of the Labour government's intention to continue the thrust of the Thatcher reforms. The league tables have been criticised on the grounds that they do not show the quality of the inputs, just the outputs, and thus may give a misleading impression. For example, if a hospital has a high death rate but a high input of chronically ill patients, then in terms of the quality of its treatments it may be as good as or better than a hospital with a low death rate but few chronically ill patients.

The private health care sector grew under Thatcher and a number of private health insurers saw growth in consequence, most notably BUPA, which not only provides private health care insurance but also has a national chain of private hospitals. Patients are choosing to go private for treatment to avoid the NHS waiting lists. Increasingly they simply pay from their own finances for this service rather than using private insurance; this 'self-pay' phenomenon is one of the most important developments in health service provision. It has come about through a combination of rising real per capita incomes and the fact that as most of us need hospital treatment only rarely, it is often affordable out of accumulated private savings.

Conclusion

The NHS has changed and continues to change quite radically in its internal structure, with the decision-making process being decentralised, but the most basic feature of the system, that it is financed out of the general tax pool and services are free at the point of delivery, remains. The NHS is the second largest single government expenditure (after social security) and has grown in expense consistently since its inception.

Other countries do not have such a high proportion of state provision of health services, yet do spend a higher proportion of GDP on health services in total, and many have more efficient provision as a consequence. Even by the early years of this century Britain spent only £946 per head per annum on health care whereas France spent £1,400 and Germany £1,600, which is over 10 per cent of GDP, while Britain's spend was only 6.7 per cent. Within the EU only Spain, Ireland, Greece and Portugal spent less. However, the largely free-market health care system in the USA produced a spend of £2,500 per head. Since 2001 spending on the NHS has risen consistently with a target of 9.4 per cent of GDP by 2007/8, although much of this increase has gone into staff pay rather than additional service provision. Structural reform has increased productivity, but the massive additional spending, and hence increased employment, in the NHS has resulted in a countervailing fall in labour productivity. Despite all of the increased spending, trust hospitals have incurred increasing debt. But the reassurance of comprehensive health care provision means that it is unlikely any British government will change the basic system.

8

Education policies

Introduction

State education, like the National Health Service, was a product of the post-war welfare state. Never before had Britain had an all-encompassing system of publicly funded primary and secondary education with services provided free at the point of delivery and financed out of the general tax pool. Further and higher education saw major expansion after the war, with much state financing as well.

School education

R. A. Butler, the Secretary of State for Education in the war-time coalition government, created the basis of the post-war state secondary education system. Following his 1944 Education Act, for the first time such education would be provided free by the state, the school leaving age would be raised from fourteen to fifteen, and the Church would be engaged in education provision. State secondary education was to be provided in a tripartite system of secondary modern, technical and grammar schools. At the age of eleven all state pupils were subject to a selection examination known as the 11-plus, an IQ test which was intended to discriminate between pupils with essentially practical skills and those with intellectual skills.

The private school system of fee-paying primary or preparatory schools and secondary or 'public' schools functioned concurrently with the state system. Enjoying charitable status and the tax advantages which go with it, the system offered high quality education at high cost to the parents. Its close association with the elite universities of Oxford and Cambridge led the civil service (and Parliament) to draw disproportionately from it: of the eleven post-war Prime Ministers, only three did not attend university (Churchill, Callaghan and

Major); the rest were all educated at Oxford and six of them attended public school.

Those pupils in the state sector who 'passed' the 11-plus test would gain entry either to technical schools or to grammar schools. The former were originally intended to provide the necessary skill sets for engineers and middle managers in what was still principally a manufacturing-based economy. Grammar schools offered a similar educational structure to the public schools, one highly academic in content. In the immediate post-war years pupils who passed the 11-plus took a matriculation exam at the end of their schooling; this was later replaced with the ordinary level (O-level) of the General Certificate of Education (GCE), which consisted of exams in each of several subjects of study taken at sixteen years of age. These schools had 'sixth forms' for optional further study; pupils who stayed at school took GCE advanced level (A-level) exams in fewer subjects at the age of eighteen.

Those pupils who 'failed' the 11-plus test were allocated to secondary modern schools, where they received basic education principally in the three Rs, plus practical education applicable to trades. In the immediate post-war years the matriculation exam was not open to those who failed the 11-plus. However, subsequently such pupils were to take Certificate of Secondary Education (CSE) exams at sixteen years of age in each subject of study, and also had the option of taking the more advanced GCE in selected subjects. These schools did not have sixth forms as no further education was expected. Pupils could elect to leave school at fifteen prior to these exams if they so wished, though from 1971 the national school-leaving age was raised to sixteen.

Schools in the state sector were given a spatial monopoly, known as a catchment area; pupils resident in that area would be sent to one of the schools in it. This created some property market distortion, as families would endeavour to purchase properties in catchment areas for those schools which had developed a good reputation for educational standards and discipline.

By the 1960s there was increasing disquiet in the Labour Party particularly regarding the philosophical rectitude of the 11-plus system, as some 80 per cent of pupils were failing it. Clearly the test was not always discriminating efficiently, and there was some evidence that it was discriminating on a class basis, as far more pupils from working-class backgrounds failed the test than did those from middle-class backgrounds. Also it was not at all clear whether any system of selection could efficiently discriminate between the life chances of pupils at an age as early as eleven.

The Labour government of Harold Wilson thus decided to abolish the 11-plus test together with the tripartite system and replace it with a unitary 'comprehensive' education system. The secondary modern, technical, and grammar schools were to be converted into comprehensive schools and all state pupils were to attend such schools without an entry examination. These schools were to retain their spatial monopolies. The Secretary of State for Education, Anthony Crosland, was charged with this responsibility in 1965. However, the problem was that local authorities, not central government, were responsible for state education provision and this meant that Crosland was obliged to publish a circular requesting, rather than demanding, that local authorities make this change. Crosland had one important advantage over the local authorities, however: it was he, as secretary of state, who provided the finance, and he used this as leverage to influence local authority policy.

The Conservatives were split over this issue; the one-nation Tories supported government policy but many Conservative-controlled local authorities refused to abolish grammar schools in their areas, seeing them as a way of providing middle-class pupils, whose parents could not afford to send their children to public schools, with a good-quality state education. Nevertheless, a rolling programme of conversion to comprehensive status was instituted and by 1968 some 20 per cent of state pupils were being educated in comprehensive schools. As this process continued through the 1970s it became clear that the existing final exams, which had been devised for the tripartite system, also needed to be changed, and to this end the CSE and GCE O-level exams were eventually merged in the late 1980s to create the General Certificate of Secondary Education exam (GCSE) in each subject of study. The GCE A-level exams were unaffected by this change.

At this time there were moves afoot in the Labour Party to end at least the privileged financial status of the public schools, if not to abolish them completely; however, this did not happen and these schools went on to thrive under the Thatcher government. The link between the public schools and Oxford and Cambridge Universities was criticised by the New Labour government of Tony Blair, and this government has cajoled these universities into accepting more state pupils.

Margaret Thatcher wished to reform state secondary education to improve efficiency with the same quasi-market system which her government would employ in the NHS (see Chapter 7). To this end the Conservatives introduced the 1988 Education Act. In order to decentralise the decision-making process, they created the Local Management of Schools (LMS), which led to grant-maintained schools, where schools in which the majority of parents voted in favour could apply to the Department of Education to manage their own affairs and no longer be subject to the line management of local education authorities. This was a very political decision as well as an economic one. During the period of the Thatcher governments, the electorate increasingly used local authority elections as referendums on national government performance, and increasingly they became Labour Party controlled. Thus LMS would wrest control of participating schools from Labour Party control.

LMS or grant-maintained status turned schools into quasi-businesses, with the teaching staff acting as the management, the head teacher as the chief executive and the board of governors as the board of directors. This decentralised the decision-making process and meant that the school was ultimately run by its board of governors, which usually comprised local people with conservative views. Funding came directly from the Department of Education, so the system was still financed out of the general tax pool with services provided free at the point of delivery.

So as to further facilitate competition between schools the spatial monopolies or catchment areas were abolished and funding provided on the basis of pupil numbers. Thus parents could choose to send their children to the schools with the best reputation for educational standards and discipline, a system called 'open enrolment'. However, there are of course limits to the short-run expansion of the best-performing schools in terms of their infrastructure capacity. The assumption was that the competitive advantages of LMS would force all schools in the state sector to apply for this status. Underperforming schools would, in the limiting case, be closed.

A compulsory system of testing was introduced to reveal pupil performance throughout their schooling. A national curriculum was also introduced to create national standards. This to some extent cut across the move towards decentralisation and diversity to meet consumer demand which the thrust of policy was intended to achieve.

School performance league tables were introduced in the 1992 Education Act to create the conditions for consumer sovereignty to function. The parents act as the agent of the child and these performance tables provide information for the parent to discriminate between schools on the basis of exam results. These tables have been criticised on the grounds that they do not convey any *value added* in the education process. With secondary schools, for example, if the quality of the input (from primary schools) is high, then a league table based on exam performance (outcomes) will give a distortedly high interpretation of the school's performance. Some table comparing inputs with outputs is needed to overcome this problem, and this could be achieved through use of the extensive system of testing for pupils introduced by the Thatcher reforms. Another problem with tables is that a child's education is not entirely determined by the teachers' performance: children learn from parents and from older siblings, and also in some cases from private tutors. Also it is tempting for schools to fail to enter poorly performing pupils for some exams so as to avoid adversely affecting the school's league table results.

To create some differentiation in the provision of secondary education and to generate further competition within the state secondary sector the Thatcher government devised city technology colleges, of which fifteen were built between 1988 and 1993. These were well-resourced secondary schools with a science and technology bias and vocationally oriented courses. They received sponsorship from private sector organisations and enjoyed a high degree of autonomy. Also the assisted places scheme was introduced, which gave government funding to pupils from deprived backgrounds who demonstrated the aptitude for a public school education. The Labour government under Tony Blair would abolish the assisted places scheme on the grounds that it was divisive and so inconsistent with its desire for social inclusion. Labour would also abolish LMS or grant-maintained schools on the grounds that such a two-tier system of schools was also divisive, and that anyway only 18 per cent of secondary schools and 3 per cent of primary schools had converted to grant-maintained status. However, Labour would reverse its position in order to improve school standards and the notion of decentralised decision-making in schools would become an important part of the party's education policy.

The Blair government introduced city academies, schools which are well resourced and have private sponsors who can donate up to £2 million, with central government providing the remainder. They enjoy wide-ranging autonomy, being able to set their own curriculum, as well as setting pay and conditions and controlling their own assets, although they are subject to a system of national standards and come within the auspices of a government trust. They constitute a development of the Conservative government policy of decentralising and removing the influence of local authorities. Other schools in the state system were to model themselves upon the academies and were also to have independence from local authority control. The government's target was to have 200 city academies in place by 2010.

However, by the autumn of 2005 the Blair government had decided to go further and announced that all secondary schools were to become independent, self-governing academies or trust schools by 2010. Parents were to be given the authority to determine the curriculum, to replace the head teachers of failing schools and to create brand new schools themselves if they wished. Local authorities were to lose their responsibility for schools, which was to be transferred instead to selected businesses, churches, City livery companies and wealthy individuals. Also, schools currently in the independent sector were to be encouraged to accept state finance. Students were to be grouped by ability and advanced classes provided for better students. However, this policy has incurred much opposition from the left of the Labour Party, their particular concern being about such schools introducing pupil selection, some sort of new 11-plus exam, and the lack of supervision by local education authorities. This has resulted in some compromise by Blair, who has offered local authorities more influence and safeguards against selection.

Further and higher education

A tertiary sector of technical colleges had existed prior to the Second World War, providing education beyond the age of sixteen; these were gradually replaced by further education colleges, many of which are state financed. These colleges provide A-level and other courses, some of which are vocational, such as Ordinary and Higher National Certificates and Diplomas (ONCs, HNCs, ONDs and HNDs) and more recently National Vocational Qualifications (NVQs). However, the value of some of these vocational courses has been questioned in regard to their applicability to work.

Like secondary schooling, higher education was also a tripartite system at the end of the Second World War, with universities, polytechnics and teacher-training colleges, the latter subsequently becoming colleges of higher education. In 1962 a full grant system was introduced, where tuition fees were paid by local authorities, as were means-tested maintenance grants, except for students over twenty-five years of age who had their entire university costs grant financed. This system was introduced by a Conservative government who could justify it on the grounds that it enabled students from an impoverished background to enjoy a university education. But as most university students were from the middle classes, the policy actually subsidised traditional Conservative voters. The university system was relatively small and grew only slowly until the 1960s, when six new campus universities were built on the American model, alongside an expansion of the metropolitan universities and the creation of the open-access Open University by the Wilson government.

In addition to the highly academic universities, there was a network of polytechnics, which evolved before the Second World War to provide the vocational education necessary to provide the skill sets demanded by manufacturing industry. However, as the manufacturing sector declined, these institutions increasingly competed with the universities by offering similar degree courses (supervised by a central polytechnic degree awarding organisation), but had to offer lower entry requirements to attract students.

When it became a requirement for secondary school teachers to have a degree, the teacher-training colleges increasingly converted to colleges of higher education in order to provide degree courses. But to attract more students they increasingly offered an ever wider range of degree courses (offered 'externally' at these colleges by universities) to students not intending a teaching career. Thus they competed with both universities and polytechnics for students, and so their entry qualifications generally became the lowest.

The proportion of students going on to higher education increased substantially during the post-war years: it was 5 per cent in 1960, but rose to 30 per cent by 1995. Thus the cost of financing this student population through the full grant system was becoming prohibitively expensive. In consequence, in 1990 a student loan scheme was introduced which provides loans to finance students in higher education and which requires graduates to repay these loans at a real interest rate (adjusted for inflation) of zero. The intended purpose of this degree of subsidy is to ensure good access to higher education for those from disadvantaged backgrounds. The loans become repayable on graduation by students when their salary exceeds £15,000, although this repayment can be deferred if the graduate's salary is less than 85 per cent of average earnings. This is to enable those who wish to take up socially useful but low-paid employment, and is also for those women who wish to leave employment to have children. The system is administered by the Student Loans Company, which provides the loans and collects the repayments. Universities can also award bursaries and scholarships to students on a contingent basis ranging in value between £300 and £3,000 a year (on average £1,000 a year). These are not repayable and are provided additionally to any money received from the government.

The Major government abolished the tripartite system in higher education, and this resulted in the rapid relabelling of polytechnics and colleges of higher education as (new) universities. From 1991 teaching and research were given separate funding systems. Funds for research were offered through a four-yearly Research Assessment Exercise. Funds for teaching were provided on a competitive basis to teach a specified number of students in each university. Universities which wanted additional funds in order to teach additional students were required to make bids to the funding bodies, though funding would be provided at a lower rate. The purpose of this competitive procedure was to increase efficiency, so the funding bodies would select bids on the basis of teaching at a low cost per student. As universities could attract more funding by teaching more students, the relatively impoverished new universities enrolled the majority of the additional students. This resulted in a fall in entry qualifications. The increase in students was so large that in 1996 the government reimposed limits on student numbers.

The Blair Labour government has continued the policy of expansion and has a target of 50 per cent of young people going on to higher education. Because of the increased size of the university student population the government also introduced university 'top-up' fees. From September 2006 universities are able to charge new full-time students up to an additional £3,000 a year in tuition fees, with this figure rising after 2010. To partially offset this increased student cost the government has provided an additional tranche of finance through the student loan scheme: for students whose parents have a household income of £17,500 or less, there is a refund on the top-up fees, with the government providing £2,700 and the university the remaining £300. Where students have a parental household income greater than this figure there is a subsidy tapering to zero at a household income of £37,400. Funds on top of these are available for disabled students and students with dependent children.

Student applications for university courses in England in 2006 saw a decline as a consequence of the introduction of the top-up system. Applications for universities in Scotland and Wales, where the Scottish Parliament and Welsh Assembly have not introduced this system, have risen.

Conclusion

The state primary and secondary education systems have been subject to quite radical reform since the end of the Second World War, with the decision-making processes being decentralised to a more local level. This has been combined with an increasing overall budget, up to £35.4 billion in 2004/5, yet according to exam league tables, standards of performance have hardly risen at all in recent years, largely because the increased spending has principally gone on raising teacher salaries.

In higher education the expansion towards a student population of 50 per cent of young people has resulted in universities trawling ever further down the A-level grades in order to attract students, with some universities now offering places without any A-level entry requirement at all. Also, many of these students are studying for qualifications with little application to the world of work. High educational standards are a necessary condition for realising a more productive workforce and so a more efficient economy, but it is not clear that the developments in higher education are achieving this.

9

The housing market and housing policies

Introduction

The housing market and housing policy have been important to the economy because of the very high proportion of national wealth which is embodied in the housing stock. Since 1945 the two best-performing investments have been the stock market and the housing market, and, given the risk-averse nature of the British, it is the housing market where so many British people have kept so much of their wealth.

The housing market in Britain is unusual by comparison with the other principal industrial economies in that there is a high proportion of private owner occupation. This has significant ramifications for economic management as it affects the monetary transmission mechanism in a fundamental way. This is discussed at some length below. But first let us consider the principal developments in British housing policy.

Housing policy

Before the First World War, approximately 90 per cent of the British housing market was composed of private rented accommodation, a substantial proportion of which was not maintained to high standards. As with much pioneering work with regard to the welfare state, it was the last Liberal government of David Lloyd George (albeit in coalition with the Conservatives) which was responsible for introducing the state provision of housing. The Housing Act of 1919 created the statutory obligation for local authorities to provide subsidised housing for low-income families, which is what became known as 'council housing'. Some housing was built under this Act in the inter-war years, but it was, as ever, Clement Attlee's Labour government after the Second World War which stimulated this policy.

One-quarter of the total housing stock had been damaged or destroyed in the war, and thousands of British people had no option in its immediate aftermath but to squat. As a consequence, to provide short-term relief, 156,000 prefabricated houses were erected in four years. Resource constraints prevented significant new construction, but with economic recovery in the 1950s the build rate of local authority and owner-occupied housing grew under both Conservative and Labour governments. Thus housing policy became part of the post-war consensus. Local authority housing had constituted barely 13 per cent of the total housing stock after the war, but by the mid-1960s this had more than doubled to nearly 30 per cent.

The 1946 Housing Act saw the creation of eight 'new towns', built on green field sites. This notion of a new town was already well established, New Lanark having been brought into existence as far back as 1816, and the better-known Welwyn Garden City in 1920. But these had been built by private entrepreneurs, whereas now new towns were to be public policy. For some years there had been migration out of the crowded urban areas into the commuter belt to escape the industrial pollution and enjoy the health-giving properties of clean country air, and new towns were to provide additional facility for this migration. Under the 1946 Act a New Town Development Corporation (a statutory body) was to be formed for each project with central government undertaking planning, finance and development. Planning for new towns was to ensure the appropriate mix of employment and shopping facilities as well as housing. Government consent was required ab initio for the acquisition of land on the open market or occasionally by compulsory purchase. The corporation would receive income from the private sector when housing was sold to owner occupiers and from land rents. When overall development was completed, the corporation would be dissolved and another body, the Commission for New Towns, would undertake the estate management functions.

The Attlee Labour government was committed to improving the housing stock by demolishing slum housing, particularly back-to-back housing, much of which was in poor condition and had outside toilets, though many larger Victorian properties were also demolished. These were replaced by a mix of high-rise local authority flats and low-rise housing. Many of the former gained a poor reputation for crime and vandalism and when the lifts were vandalised it created problems of access. Also, the lack of a garden was disliked by tenants. Although much of this housing stock was built to adequate standards, there were a few spectacular partial collapses of tower blocks because of faulty build quality. As a result, and because of financial constraints on government, by the 1960s there was a slowdown in the local authority building programme and so the proportion of the housing stock provided by local authorities remained roughly static at just under 30 per cent from the 1960s through to the early 1980s. Constraints on local authority finance, combined with the fact that subsidised rents provided authorities with only a meagre income stream from this source, meant that local authorities were not receiving sufficient funds to provide proper maintenance. Thus by 1980 it was estimated that nearly £20 billion was needed for repair and refurbishment of the public housing stock.

The problems of high-rise housing led to a change of policy by the 1980s, when some of the tower blocks were themselves demolished and emphasis shifted to low-rise housing with 'defensible space'. This is the notion that, unlike high-rise flats where communal access is right up to the front doors, low-rise dwellings, with small gardens or front doors set back, create a psychological barrier for passers-by, because of the quasi-private space in front of the dwellings. This has been shown to reduce crime and vandalism and make for more agreeable living conditions.

The Thatcher housing policy shifted the emphasis from subsidising local authority provision of housing to subsidising the demand for housing and to targeting the poorest families. In 1982 housing benefit was introduced, which incorporated rent rebates, and the 1988 Social Security Act provided this benefit to low-income families to enable them to rent either local authority or private housing. However, the cost of housing benefit was high, as nearly two-thirds of local authority tenants were in receipt of it, and the recession of the early 1990s made this worse (see Chapter 5). The net result was that five years after the 1988 Act, the total cost of housing benefit had risen from over £3.5 billion to nearly £8.5 billion. Also, a 'housing trap' had developed: because housing benefit was withdrawn as incomes grew, families could not afford to improve their accommodation. Housing benefit also had a detrimental effect on the market mechanism, as those receiving the benefit in the private sector had no incentive to shop around for housing in order to drive down rents, or accept more modest accommodation.

It was hoped that the fact that rents were no longer being subsidised would mean that the increased revenue from them to both the public and the private sectors would provide sufficient funds to ensure high-quality maintenance. In the public sector, rental income to local authorities from this source in England increased by two and a half times in the ten years from 1979 to stand at over £3 billion. But this was accompanied by a reduction of more than 80 per cent in housing subsidy to £240 million.

As part of Thatcher's overall policy of trying to reduce the size of the state, the 1980 Housing Act also required local authorities to sell off existing housing stock to sitting tenants at a subsidised rate – the 'right-to-buy' policy – and forbade the local authorities from constructing replacement housing. In fact, this policy had already been tried by the Heath government in 1970, when local authorities could sell at a 20 per cent discount, but there was little take up. In 1980, in order to encourage tenants to buy, the dwellings were sold at prices between a half and two-thirds of their market value, contingent on the duration of the tenancy. Local authorities offered mortgages to finance this, though nearly two-thirds of purchasers would actually go to the building societies. Sales grew quickly, peaking at more than 200,000 per annum just a couple of years after the policy was introduced, then gradually falling towards the end of the decade. By the time New Labour were in government, in excess of 1.6 million dwellings had been sold, more than a quarter of the stock, leaving fewer than 4.9 million still in public ownership.

The right-to-buy policy reduced the proportion of local authority housing provision still further, and so augmented private housing ownership. Consequently, the proportion of local authority housing in the total housing stock fell from just under 30 per cent in the early 1980s to barely more than half that by the end of the century.

It was clearly recognised that it was not possible for all housing needs to be provided by the free market alone, and given the decline in the provision of local authority accommodation, the housing needs of the lowest income groups in society needed to be addressed in a new way. It would be housing associations which would perform this function. Housing associations are voluntary not-for-profit private sector organisations; they have significant public sector finance but enjoy some income from the private sector and most importantly, at least from the perspective of the Conservatives, they were not directly controlled by what were increasingly Labour-dominated local authorities. This lack of local authority control would also appeal to the New Labour government of Tony Blair!

Housing associations were by no means new, but dated back to the 1960s. The original intention in creating them was to offer a specialist service for the elderly and disabled and to finance the redevelopment of inner-city housing, which had suffered from urban decay. They are financed and audited by the Housing Corporation, an organisation which receives half its finance from central government, some of the rest being provided by local authorities, but some also by private financial institutions, the construction sector and through raising finance on the capital markets. Housing associations have now become the central plank of policy for providing social housing, and central government finance for them has been increased and borrowing restrictions eased in consequence. Also, some local authorities have transferred the remainder of their housing stock to housing associations. By 2005 there were in excess of 1,500 such associations in England, with approximately two million homes housing more than 4 million people They have the novelty of allowing tenants to purchase an increasing proportion of the equity in their homes when their finances allow, with the rental liability diminishing as their equity increases. This means, of course, that tenants can purchase their homes outright eventually when their finances permit.

A new problem in the housing market arose in the early 1990s which became known as negative equity. This occurs when where a fall in property prices results in a property having a lesser value than the mortgage secured on it. This situation resulted from the economic recession of the late 1980s and early 1990s (see Chapter 5). Property prices were to begin falling in the autumn of 1989 and to continue to do so until 1994, by which time aggregate negative equity had accrued to about £7.5 billion. At its worst average house prices were falling at some 17 per cent per annum, with annual 30 per cent falls in what were for the Conservative government the politically sensitive areas of London and south-east England. It was an important political issue as the electorate were unaccustomed to losing money on property sales, and so became a factor in the defeat of the Conservatives at the 1997 general election. This was despite the fact that property prices had started to rise again due to the growth of the economy after the European Monetary System debacle (see Chapter 5), which consequently eliminated negative equity by the time of the election.

Because of growing national wealth and concerns about pensions (see Chapter 6), the housing market became part of private pension provision. Mature people with accumulated savings began to invest in property to rent out: the 'buy-to-let' market. Because of the potential returns, people are increasingly taking out mortgages to get into this market. This provides both an income stream to the owners and augments their wealth through the capital growth of the property. Consequently this has helped to raise house prices further and increased the proportion of housing in private ownership. The Conservative policy towards local authority housing resulted in a growing shortage of accommodation for the homeless, and paradoxically this has resulted in local authorities renting property from the buy-to-let market at market prices, in some cases the very housing which was sold off under the right to buy!

When New Labour came to power, housing policy was first transferred from the Department of the Environment to the then newly created Department of the Environment, Transport and the Regions (see Chapter 10), with the deputy Prime Minister, John Prescott, as secretary of state. Then when this department was abolished, housing policy was transferred to the Office of the Deputy Prime Minister, still under Prescott. He was responsible for introducing the Housing Act of 2004 and proposed spending £38 billion on housing expansion. The Act includes a requirement, from 2007, for those wishing to sell property to provide a 'home information pack' containing a home condition report, to shift the cost of surveying the property from buyers to sellers. The Act also reduces the scope for tenants to purchase their dwellings under the right-to-buy scheme at a subsidised rate and then to resell them at the market rate. Local authorities are given powers to prevent anti-social tenants from purchasing their dwellings under the right-to-buy scheme. The Act also increases the regulations covering landlords and protects private tenants' deposits.

Tenure

Owner occupation stood at 10 per cent of the total housing stock before the First World War, and approximately 25 per cent after the Second World War, but it grew substantially from the late 1950s to stand at approximately 70 per cent in the early twenty-first century, equating to some 17 million dwellings, higher than in most industrial societies. Owner-occupiers see housing as an 'investment good', and a culture of owner occupation has developed in consequence. As part of this culture young people aspire to owner occupation, and as property prices rise there is an incentive 'to get on to the housing ladder' before prices become out of reach. House prices increase and so people enjoy a rise in their personal wealth which is both unearned and untaxed.*A very high proportion of owner-occupied housing, and thus national wealth, is therefore embodied in the housing stock.

Owner occupation was partly fuelled by the fact that there is no capital gains tax payable on owner-occupied dwellings (unless they are second

* Stamp duty & IHT may be factors

homes) and by mortgage interest tax relief or MIRAS (mortgage interest relief at source). Under this scheme, the incidence of tax on mortgage interest repayments was reduced deliberately to encourage owner occupation. In 1974 this was limited by the Labour government to the first £25,000 borrowed, but it was raised in 1983 to £30,000 by the Conservatives largely to index it with house price inflation. In 1991 the Conservatives constrained MIRAS to the basic rate of income tax, but it was then progressively reduced in stages to 10 per cent in 1999 and finally abolished by the Labour government in April 2000.

Until the deregulation of the financial services sector in 1986 (see below), the provision of mortgages was by the building societies only. These received funds from the public by offering interest on private savings accounts, and these funds were then loaned out at interest to owner-occupiers to purchase their dwellings. This financial structure had an inherent flaw, namely that building societies were borrowing short term and lending long term, for savings provided by the public tend to stay in building society accounts only for short periods, but building society loans (mortgages) are long term, perhaps twenty-five years. This made the building societies inherently cautious in their mortgage-lending activities, and consequently restricted the availability of mortgages. The emphasis was to lend to professional people in full-time employment who could expect promotion and thus incremental increases in their salaries, and who wished to purchase freehold, brick-built three-bedroom houses. Thus, demand for mortgages exceeded supply and those without the foregoing qualities found it hard to obtain mortgages at all.

In 1915, Herbert Asquith's Liberal government introduced the Increase of Rent and Mortgage (War Restrictions) Act. This was intended as a temporary measure to protect rents at the 1914 level, and it also introduced security of tenure for tenants. However, it was not repealed after the First World War but was to form part of housing policy up until the 1980s. The Conservative government's Rent Act of 1957 introduced some deregulation, but during the 1950s and 1960s there were a number of scandals concerning landlords who were responsible for poor quality maintenance and exploitative rents (most notably Peter Rachman), and so the Labour government of Harold Wilson repealed the 1957 Act.

In 1977 Labour under James Callaghan introduced a new Rent Act, under which a 'fair rent' for tenants would be determined by a rent officer or a rent assessment committee. The Act provided security of tenure for the existing tenant, and then for two subsequent tenants, but only if they had been living in the dwelling with their predecessors for at least six months. This usually applied to family members, either a spouse or children.

By 1978 government expenditure constraints resulted in the imposition of restrictions on local authority spending, in consequence of which the proportion of local authority housing expenditure which the authorities were permitted to cover by borrowing was reduced progressively from 100 per cent. The Thatcher government wanted to constrain local authority expenditure as part of its overall economic policy and so by the end of the 1980s this proportion had been reduced to under a quarter.

With a growing owner-occupier market, yet rent controls on private rented housing, landlords achieved a higher rate of return by selling their private rented stock to the owner-occupied sector and investing outside the housing market. As a result the private rented sector contracted drastically. Private rented accommodation accounted for nearly two-thirds of the housing market after the Second World War, but this had fallen to less than a third twenty years later and to roughly one-tenth by the mid 1980s. With local authorities providing subsidised housing, and a falling supply of private rented accommodation, the demand for local authority housing persistently exceeded supply; the net result of this was waiting lists for such housing. This had to be addressed by prioritising those in housing need, with young single parents enjoying priority over other groups. Also, the statutory requirement for local authorities to house the homeless meant that bed-and-breakfast accom- modation had to be rented by local authorities to provide sufficient housing.

As the Thatcher government believed in free-market solutions, it decided to reverse the decline in the private rented sector. The 1980 Housing Act introduced market-determined rents, but did keep secure tenure for new properties except for tenancies with a short fixed term. The 1988 Housing Act deregulated rents for all tenancies, thus raising rates of return for landlords and so encouraging increased supply. By the end of the 1980s average rents had trebled in ten years. The Act also introduced assured tenancy and assured shorthold tenancy agreements, which came into force in January 1989. Assured tenancies gave the landlord the option of renewing or terminating the tenancy agreement after a fixed period, though if disputed it often required a court to decide if the agreement should be terminated. Assured shorthold tenancies gave the landlord the right to terminate the agreement after six months, and failure to vacate the premises by the tenant required a court to enforce termination. In order to further develop the free market, the 1996 Housing Act codified shorthold tenancies as the standard agreement and abolished the six-month minimum term. Landlords had already predominantly opted for shorthold tenancies anyway as they gave them superior rights. Tenants who had signed agreements prior to the 1988 Act enjoyed (and continue to enjoy) the provisions of the 1977 Act.

House prices and their effect on GDP

With the developments in the British housing market mentioned above, the monetary transmission mechanism between interest rate policy and gross domestic product (GDP) has changed in a fundamental way. Traditional text book theory tells us that the monetary transmission mechanism functions causally from central bank interest rate changes via private interest-sensitive expenditure (principally investment) to GDP. But as we shall see below, increasingly the monetary transmission mechanism is functioning via the housing market. Of course it has long been understood that a change in monetary policy causes a change in mortgage repayments, which in turn causes changes in disposable income, and thus consumption and so GDP. However, there are other causal linkages which have become increasingly important.

House prices are causally correlated with GDP via the following three discrete transmission mechanisms. Firstly, changes in consumer optimism cause the demand for housing and in turn house prices to change, thus there is a positive correlation between consumer optimism and house price changes. The foregoing also causes the demand for consumption goods and so their prices to change, again a positive correlation, so house prices and consumption goods prices tend to move together. As consumption changes, so does GDP.

Secondly, as house prices are positively correlated with the quantity of housing transactions, there is a positive causal correlation between the demand for housing and the demand for, and thus prices of, household durable goods (washing machines, TV sets, etc.). Durable-good consumption tends to change by more than non-durable-good consumption.

The third mechanism is perhaps the most significant, and also the most recent, development; it concerns a notion called mortgage equity withdrawal (MEW). This occurs because rising house prices cause a rise in household wealth. Householders undertake additional borrowing from the mortgage provider, raising the value of the mortgage, sometimes up to the new value of the dwelling. The additional borrowing is employed to augment current consumption and therefore affects GDP.

An unanticipated fall in interest rates will bring about a change in GDP in the following way. MEW, as a secured loan, incurs a lower interest rate than unsecured loans, thus MEW not only raises the demand for, and thus the prices of, consumption goods, but raises those prices by a greater magnitude than if the loans were unsecured. The transmission mechanism is thus from house price rises to GDP via MEW and consumption.

The transaction costs of MEW have fallen since the early 1990s, and further developments in the financial service industry are likely to reduce this further. This has and will continue to have the effect *ceteris paribus* of increasing the aggregate quantity of MEW. Prior to the 1980s there was little opportunity to undertake MEW; during this period, as we have already seen, mortgages were supplied by building societies and their provision was rationed. MEW could only be achieved by moving house, so discharging the existing mortgage and taking out a new one, which naturally incurred high transaction costs. New mortgage products have permitted additional borrowing (MEW) at virtually zero transaction costs. The increased demand for these more versatile mortgages indicates that their supply is likely to continue to rise.

So how is this affecting the behaviour of house prices, consumption and so GDP? Assume an unanticipated interest rate cut: the effect on consumption is large relative to the effect on housing demand and so on house prices. This is because households undertake MEW and so increase their consumption by a greater magnitude than in the past to a given change in house prices.

The 1986 Building Societies Act removed constraints restricting the products which building societies were able to offer. This deregulation enabled them to act as banks, and so increased the availability of credit. One range of products they introduced was unsecured credit, thus increasing the availability of such products in the market, and reducing their transaction costs. Also, there were non-bank entrants into the credit market, including a range of retailers such as department stores as well as insurance companies. These provide unsecured loans, mortgages and credit cards.

The decision whether to undertake additional unsecured borrowing is partly related to housing wealth: if housing wealth rises, households will *ceteris paribus* feel more secure about undertaking increased unsecured debt. Unsecured credit acts directly on consumption and so on GDP.

We can divide up households into two discrete categories:

- Those subject to the permanent income hypothesis, where consumption decisions are based on expected total lifetime income, who will vary consumption when expectations of future income vary.

- Those whose consumption patterns are positively correlated with short-term fluctuations in personal income, that is, those who vary consumption as they receive a pay rise or lose a job.

Household consumption patterns in the second category react by a greater magnitude to changes in current income than those of the first-category households. The Institute for Fiscal Studies has shown that there has been an increase in the proportion of households in the second category in the economy. As the proportion of this category rises in the economy, the response of consumption and so GDP to interest rate changes increases relative to changes in housing demand and house prices. Thus, an unanticipated interest rate fall will cause a larger rise in consumption and so inflation relative to the rise in housing demand and housing prices.

The increase in the availability of credit means that consumers do not have significantly to reduce consumption if incomes fall (as they can borrow more), particularly if consumers expect any fall in income to be only temporary. This may be because people tend to be subject to 'cognitive dissonance'; in other words, consumers are subjectively more likely to believe that a fall in income is temporary than objective empirical evidence would indicate. Thus changes in consumption and GDP tend not to be influenced as much by income changes as they did in the past.

So we can sum up that as the quantity of MEW has risen in recent years, and as access to other forms of credit has concurrently become easier, therefore, for a given increase in house prices, the rate of additional borrowing spent on non-housing consumption compared to that spent on additional housing demand is greater than in the past. Thus consumption and so GDP will change much more in response to an unanticipated fall in interest rates than was the case in the past. Monetary policy is thus significantly influencing household wealth and hence consumption and GDP. This is due to the deregulation of the mortgage market and of the market for unsecured loans, as well as by the very large and growing proportion of home ownership in Britain. This is highly significant for macroeconomic policy, as the monetary transmission mechanism is increasingly acting via the housing market.

However, a more disquieting phenomenon is the fall in the savings ratio as the nation spends ever more of its wealth. This has occurred not simply because debt levels have risen, but because, as an ever higher proportion of national wealth is embodied in the housing stock, less is embodied in savings which constitute investment funds for the productive sector of the economy. The problem is that housing is in fact a 'consumption good' and so not part of either savings or investment. This change may be causing investment to be less sensitive to unanticipated interest rate changes and therefore *ceteris paribus* dampening consumption and GDP changes. If this change continues indefinitely then the productive sector of the economy will be adversely affected.

Conclusion

The composition of the British housing market has changed fundamentally since 1945 with the dramatic growth of owner occupation, the expansion and then to some extent contraction of local authority housing, and the fall and then rise in private rented accommodation. Some of this is accounted for by policy, but the growth of owner occupation, although partly driven by policy, has been principally driven by a desire to have a secure repository for personal wealth. But the housing market is not simply a welfare issue, with housing policy being part of social policy; rather it has increasingly developed into one of great significance for economic policy more broadly. As with the NHS, Britain is unique in this matter.

10

Transport policies

Introduction

Britain's transport structure is largely determined by the geography of the nation. The relatively short distances to be travelled have meant that historically a network of comparatively small roads developed in an ad hoc way, later complemented by a complex rail service offering mostly short but frequent services. With the decline of the rail network since the Second World War, successive governments embarked on a road-building and improvement policy and created the motorway network. However, there has been increased congestion on both road and rail. With a high population density it is expensive to develop new transport services as urban sprawl offers so many barriers.

Air travel, both domestic and international, has grown massively since 1945, particularly from the 1960s, by which time the growth in real per capita incomes, together with advances in aeronautical technology, allowed ordinary people to travel by air. Passenger shipping saw a decline during the same period, but merchant shipping would undergo a revolution through the 'containerisation' of freight transportation.

After the Second World War the Labour government of Clement Attlee was to nationalise much of the British transport system. On 1 January 1948 the British Transport Commission (BTC) was formed, which included executives created to run British Railways, London Transport, the inland waterways (including the canals) and the docks. Later that year, executive committees for road transport and hotels were also set up. In 1953 the Conservative government of Winston Churchill introduced a Transport Act which would privatise or abolish all of these executives with the exception of the London Transport Executive. The Conservative government of Harold Macmillan then introduced the 1962 Transport Act, which abolished the BTC and replaced it with government-appointed, though independent, management boards. British Railways, renamed British Rail in 1968, would be privatised in the 1990s. The Labour government of Clement Attlee also nationalised long-distance road freight haulage after the war, but this was denationalised by the Conservatives in the 1950s.

Rail

British Railways was created by the post-war Labour government's decision to nationalise the four big private rail companies (the Great Western Railway, the London, Midland and Scottish Railway, the London and North Eastern Railway and the Southern Railway) and was a policy based on socialist ideology. By state ownership of the assets it was expected that commercial exploitation of the workforce would be eliminated, and services would be provided on the basis of social need rather than profit. In fact, although the four big rail companies that preceded nationalisation were private companies, they had been brought into existence in 1923 as the direct result of govern-ment policy. War-time policy amounted to a virtual nationalisation of the rail network anyway and so formal nationalisation was a natural step. It was hoped that centralising locomotive and rolling stock design and production, as well as administration, would lead to some economies of scale. But operating a railway is always expensive because of the high fixed costs. This means that costs are covered by revenues only on the high-density commuter services during peak hours and some of the long-distance services where there is little competition. Thus massive subsidy has been necessary to finance the railway system.

Nationalisation became part of the post-war consensus but it did not prevent the long-run decline of the rail system, nor did the modernisation plan, where steam was replaced with diesel and electric traction from 1955. It is a common misconception that it was Richard Beeching's (who then ran British Railways) report in 1963 which resulted in the rail closure programme. Although this report did result in accelerated closures, which continued into the 1970s, in fact the rail network had reached its peak in about 1900, after which there was steady decline, initially because there had been speculative railway projects which proved unprofitable, but subsequently because of the inexorable rise of motorised road transport for both passengers and freight.

It was hoped that long-distance rail travel would have a prosperous future and to this end the 155mph Advanced Passenger Train (APT) was developed in the 1970s. Originally gas turbine powered and later electric powered via overhead catenary, the APT had a body-tilting mechanism to enable it to travel at high speed on the old sinuous track system, far cheaper than building a new straighter track. Failure to make the tilting mechanism work reliably meant its cancellation in 1984, leaving only the slower non-tilting train, the High Speed Train, which had been introduced in 1976 and was capable of 125mph.

The Conservative government of John Major decided to privatise British Rail in 1992. It went about this by creating a private company that owned and operated the track and signalling equipment, Railtrack, and by offering regional franchises at tender for train-operating companies (TOCs) to provide the services. Additional private firms were employed to carry out maintenance work on the infrastructure and to own and manufacture rolling stock, which was leased to the TOCs. This proved to be a complex system, the net result of which was very poor communication within the industry, which was subsequently blamed for a number of accidents.

When the New Labour government of Tony Blair came to power in 1997 it undertook focus group studies amongst the electorate to determine which policy issues to prioritise. It discovered that transport and environmental policy concerns were low on the electorate's agenda, and so decided to merge the two departments dealing with these matters. The Department of Transport and the Department of the Environment were thus merged to create the Department of the Environment, Transport and the Regions (DETR) and John Prescott, the deputy Prime Minister, was made secretary of state for the department. Prescott had been appointed deputy Prime Minister by Blair because he had influence with the left wing of the Labour Party yet subscribed to Blair's policy agenda. He lacked the intellect and judgement to be part of the core executive and so Blair gave him this new, relatively unimportant, department to manage. The DETR lasted until April 2001, when it was further reorganised into the Department for Transport, Local Government and the Regions, which in turn lasted just thirteen months until May 2002. A series of rail crashes heightened the policy profile of transport, so the government then reorganised the department yet again, and created a separate Department for Transport once more.

This series of rail crashes prompted the New Labour government to create Network Rail, not a nationalised company but a not-for-profit organisation, to take over Railtrack's responsibilities. Control of the rail system was subsequently centralised further, giving Network Rail responsibility for strategic planning across the entire rail industry as well as responsibility for timetabling and control over the maintenance of the track and signalling equipment. It had been failure of the maintenance procedures which had caused the train crashes previously. The government took responsibility for the principal agreements between all of the participating organisations in the rail industry, for determining overall public expenditure on the railways and for major purchasing decisions. The regulatory quango, the Office of Rail Regulation, oversees the latter function as well as taking responsibility for safety. Some powers are devolved to the Scottish Executive, the Welsh Assembly and the mayor of London. During this period there has been some growth in demand for rail transport as the economy has grown.

London's underground railway system, familiarly known as 'the Tube', which had been under the control of the London Passenger Transport Board since 1933, was brought under public ownership after the Second World War, but investment in the industry remained modest until the 1960s, when the first new line since 1907 was built. The Victoria line was opened in stages between 1968 and 1971, and this was followed a decade later by another new line, the Jubilee line, opened in 1979 and named after Queen Elizabeth's silver jubilee (though this had occurred two years previously). The Jubilee line was extended in 1999 to provide a link with the growing area south of the Thames and on to London's docklands.

In 1970 the responsibility for London Transport was transferred from central government to the Greater London Council (GLC) (see Chapter 3). When Ken Livingstone was elected head of the GLC in 1980, he had campaigned on a policy of introducing cheaper fares on London Transport services. He consequently introduced a policy called 'Fares fair' which reduced ticket prices by a third. The policy was financed by a supplementary rate (tax) imposed on London rate payers. 'Fares fair' only increased Tube passenger traffic by 9 per cent, which was insufficient to finance the fare reductions, and in consequence the subsidy provided for these services increased from less than a third to more than a half. However, the Conservative-controlled Bromley Borough Council, on the outskirts of London, decided to bring a court action against the GLC on the grounds that the supplementary rate as it was imposed on Bromley rate payers was not fair, as the borough did not have Tube services. The court case went all the way up to the House of Lords, and the 'Fares fair' policy was finally ruled to be illegal. In 1983 the GLC came up with a simplified system of zone pricing, creating 'Travelcards'. Two years later this scheme was expanded to cover British Rail's commuter train system into London.

In 1984 London Transport was once again brought under central government control and was replaced by London Regional Transport (LRT), a holding company controlling both buses and the Underground. Ostensibly this was on the recommendation of the House of Commons Transport Committee, but in reality it was largely a political measure carried out by the Conservative government to prevent a Labour-controlled GLC from heavily subsidising rail services, contrary to central government policy. In 2000 the New Labour government created Transport for London (TfL), which became responsible for underground rail and bus services in London. TfL is part of the Greater London Authority and is responsible to a commissioner of transport, and ultimately to the mayor of London, Ken Livingstone again.

In the 1980s the Docklands Light Railway (DLR) was created, originally as a private venture, and later incorporated into TfL. This provides rail services between central London and the commercial developments in the former London docks.

The construction of a tunnel beneath the English Channel had been first attempted in the late nineteenth century; however, technological problems aside, the project was stopped because it was feared that the French would use it as a conduit to invade England! No further serious attempt was made at a fixed link until the early 1970s, when an Anglo-French agreement initiated a rail link, but only a few metres had been constructed before lack of finance and lack of commitment saw it abandoned in 1975. The project was revived in 1984. The socialist French President, François Mitterrand, was committed to the idea of a state-financed rail link, but the neo-liberal Margaret Thatcher was opposed both to state financing and to the notion of a rail, rather than a road, link. She was persuaded that on practical grounds a tunnel of that length under water would need to be rail, but she insisted on private finance. Private commercial banks from a number of countries were cajoled into providing the finance, and with no insurmountable technical difficulties the project progressed relatively smoothly.

The purpose of the Channel Tunnel was to provide a facility for high-speed trains to run directly, city centre to city centre, between London and Paris and London and Brussels and therefore compete head on with the airlines. Also, it was intended that a motor vehicle-carrying service should operate between terminals at each end of the tunnel and thus offer direct competition with the roll-on, roll-off (ro-ro) cross-channel ferries which had operated between Dover or Folkestone and Boulogne or Calais since the 1950s.

Immediately there were difficulties arising from the state of the rail system on this side of the channel. The railway network in the south-east had grown up piecemeal since the 1840s and there was no direct high-speed line to connect the tunnel to the London terminus at Waterloo. The problem of surveying a line through the densely packed suburban areas of Kent was considerable, not to mention the difficulty in gaining planning permission to build it. By comparison, the lightly populated areas on the French side of the channel and the aggressive French system of forcing through public projects meant that trains could travel at speeds not possible on any part of the British Rail system. For years after the tunnel's completion services had to trundle at modest speeds through the Kent countryside, losing the advantage of speed to compete with the airlines. The high-speed line from the tunnel to London was not initiated until 1996 and is due to be completed in 2007, whereupon the Waterloo terminus will be replaced by one at St Pancras, on the north side of central London, to offer connecting services to the north of Britain.

With respect to the cross-channel motor vehicle transport service, the ferry companies rationalised their routes by operating between Dover and Calais only, and began to offer high-quality 'cruise liner' services to attract custom, by comparison with the Channel Tunnel trains, where you have to sit in your car. At the same time London City Airport was set up in Docklands, with very short rail and road linkages to central London. Admittedly this airport is only capable of operating small feeder liners, but it offers another level of competition. The net result is that rates of return on the Channel Tunnel services have been poor and the banks have had to write off most of the debt.

Road

Britain's road network suffered in comparison with the German autobahns built by Hitler in the 1930s and the American freeways, and it was felt after the Second World War that Britain needed to catch up. The country did not have a motorway system at all; indeed, the alignment of some of the road network, including major routes, dated back to Roman times! Britain was to inaugurate its first motorway, the M1, in 1958 and by 1971 1,000 miles of motorway had been completed. But many of the motorways, as with existing major routes, migrated out from London. This meant huge congestion as traffic navigated its way through the capital, which would not be alleviated until the M25 orbital motorway around London was completed in 1986. Today motorways and trunk routes still constitute less than 2.5 per cent of

England's roads, yet they carry nearly one-third of all traffic and up to two-thirds of freight.

Throughout the post-war years governments attempted to predict future growth in road transport, building motorways and bypasses and upgrading major routes as a consequence. In recent years various theorists such as Martin Moggeridge have argued that traffic shifts between road and rail until journey times equalise; in consequence a large road-building programme means that traffic will shift from rail to road until congestion on the roads increases journey times, and falling rail congestion reduces journey times on that network. For environmental reasons it was therefore advocated that policy should emphasise rail travel, as more road building simply attracted more traffic to the roads. It is also the case that as real per capita incomes have grown and there has been increased global car production plus technological development, this has reduced the real cost of motoring, and so more and more people have been able to afford a car.

The New Labour government of Tony Blair gave a nod to these concerns when it came to power in 1997, but when the DETR published its ten-year transport plan in 2000 it advocated more spending on all forms of transport, including roads (£11.2 billion) and rail, and some twenty-five new light rail schemes. This was perceived as a retreat from the government's green strategy and a return to the policy of predicting increased transport demand and providing capacity for it.

The increase in road traffic after the Second World War caused a rise in the incidence of accidents and this led directly both to the introduction in 1965 of a national speed limit of 70 miles per hour and to the compulsory fitting of front seatbelts in cars, with their compulsory wearing some years later.

The development of speed cameras in the 1990s for road safety and as an environmental measure to reduce emissions has accompanied a progressive increase in taxation on petrol, which by the early twenty-first century would account for some 73 per cent of the price of petrol. In both cases these constitute methods of tax revenue gathering; speeding fines have risen inexorably since the introduction of cameras, and the fact that the demand for petrol is very inelastic (if the price rises because of a tax rise, there is only a small fall in demand, so the total expenditure on petrol rises) means that it is an effective means of raising revenue for the government. Also, the incidence of parking fines has risen such that in some London boroughs parking fines plus fees charged for parking yield more revenue than the council tax. It is true that the incidence of taxation, other things being equal, reduces the use of motor cars and so has environmental benefits, but for an environmental tax to work, it has to be equal to the marginal external cost (that of the environmental damage; see Chapter 13). However, taxes are simply not set at this level in this country, partly because it is difficult to ascertain what this value is, but more importantly because the principal purpose of the tax is revenue gathering to finance government expenditure.

Bus services expanded after the Second World War with some, including London's buses (London Transport), under state ownership. The last electric trams in London were withdrawn from service in 1952 and replaced by buses. Expansion of the bus network was partly due to the railway closure programme.

By the 1980s, under the Conservative government's policy of competition, bus routes were put out to competitive tender. In the capital, both the state-owned London Buses and private companies tendered for three-year renewable contracts. In 1993 the Conservative government decided to privatise London Buses. In 2000 the Labour government brought London Buses under the control of TfL along with the Underground rail network. This organisation is now also responsible for London's entire 360-mile network of main roads and the regulation of taxis, both the traditional black cabs and other private hire vehicles. As mentioned above, the mayor of London is now responsible for TfL. The bus and Tube network is heavily subsidised principally from central government funds.

The first executive mayor of London, Ken Livingstone, intrinsically hostile to private motor vehicle transport, decided to introduce a congestion charging system for road traffic in central London. The purpose of the scheme is to increase the cost of operating private and commercial motor vehicles relative to the cost of public transport and thus shift traffic from the former to the latter. Central government subsequently picked up the idea of congestion charging and now advocates its introduction in other cities across the country.

In order for this scheme to be feasible, some very advanced technology is needed. At all of the entry points into the controlled zone fixed cameras were installed which, via computers, read the registration number of each vehicle travelling into the zone and check these against a database of owners who have paid the charge for that day. Mobile cameras operate in the zone to identify vehicles which have been parked overnight inside the zone and have subsequently travelled inside the zone only. A charge paid at various shops, by telephone, or over the internet is required from all vehicle owners (with some concessions) who wish to drive their vehicles in the zone. The system operates Monday to Friday from 7 a.m. to 6.30 p.m., excluding public holidays.

The congestion charge has reduced congestion and speeded up bus journeys, but the problem is that it is highly regressive: it is a flat rate charge which constitutes a very small proportion of the income of a senior business executive who comes into central London in his chauffeur-driven limousine, perhaps twice or three times a week, by comparison with the tradesman who needs to come into central London five days a week and who can hardly hop on a bus with all of his wares.

Air

Immediately after the Second World War, commercial aviation was reserved for the rich and for colonial civil servants travelling back and forth to the Empire. Airports were small, even London's Croydon airport, and it was still expected that the largest aircraft would be flying boats operating from coastal ports, as had been the case before the war. However, the commercial development of war-time long-range bombers would demonstrate that major new airports were needed and so Croydon was replaced as London's major airport by a new purpose-built facility at Heathrow.

Frank Whittle's invention of the jet engine would revolutionise commercial air travel, just as it had done for military aircraft. The growth in the size of jet aircraft would reduce the seat-pence-per-mile operating costs and so bring air travel within reach of many more people. But it would be the advent of package holidays by air from the late 1960s which would revolutionise air travel for the mass market. In consequence, London gained additional airports at Gatwick and later Stansted as well as Luton, and many regional airports were built. Current policy is for continued expansion with ever more terminals at Heathrow and an additional runway at Stansted. Aviation fuel is zero rated for tax, because it would require international agreement to impose tax on this fuel and this is unforthcoming. This provides air travel with a competitive advantage.

The British Overseas Airways Corporation (BOAC) and British European Airways (BEA) were this country's principal carriers after the war, though smaller independent airlines grew up as well. In 1974 BOAC and BEA merged to become British Airways (BA). BA was a nationalised industry and, measured by number of employees, was the largest airline in the Western world (although the Soviet airline, Aeroflot, was larger, and some US airlines had larger fleets). The airline was privatised in 1987 whereupon, inevitably, the number of employees fell (see also Chapter 11).

It had been British government policy after the war to identify air transport needs and to sponsor commercial aircraft development, and to that end the Brabazon Committee was set up. It identified the need for the development of a large inter-continental airliner, but stipulated in its technical specification a design philosophy which was largely pre-war. Swept wings and jet engines, which were to revolutionise post-war aviation, were not included in the design. Despite this, production of a prototype of this aircraft, to be called the Brabazon, went ahead; it flew, and a second was under construction when the whole project was abandoned at great cost to the taxpayer.

The privately developed De Havilland Comet was to be the world's first commercial jet airliner and successfully went into service in 1952. However, defects in its pressure cabin caused several crashes with the loss of all on board. The fault was rectified and the aircraft's specification was updated, but it would be American designs which would now dominate the market. This was not because of the Comet crashes, as is often falsely stated, but rather because the design of the American aircraft made them inherently cheaper to operate.

In the 1960s the government joined forces with the French and sponsored a supersonic civil aviation project, the Concorde. The French, very strong politically, would take design leadership, though the British possessed the bulk of the technology. An engineering triumph and an icon of the twentieth century, it was far too expensive for the airlines to purchase, and in the end the few which were built were given away to the two national airlines, British Airways and Air France, with the taxpayer-funded development costs written off. The Soviet Union briefly had its own supersonic airliner, the Tupolev Tu 144, in domestic service across the vast expanse of the country, but a spectacular air crash caused its withdrawal from service. The Boeing Supersonic Transport (SST) was cancelled before it ever flew, so British Airways and Air France enjoyed the monopoly of supersonic air services across the Atlantic and in consequence Concordes were operated profitably by both airlines for years until their retirement in 2003. In 2000, an Air France Concorde did crash, killing all on board, but retrospective modifications were made to all remaining Concordes to prevent a repetition, and in the end it was simply the operating economics which ended this era of supersonic civil air transport.

Sea

In 1900, Britain's merchant navy and the Royal Navy were jointly larger than all the rest of the world's navies put together, reflecting the fact that Britain had an Empire upon which the sun never set, the largest in history. To some extent this was still the case in 1945, but the dismantling of the Empire thereafter (see Chapter 12) and the relative decline of the British economy (see Chapters 5 and 11) led to a massive reduction in British merchant shipping.

The decline of maritime passenger traffic after the Second World War resulted from two principal factors: jet aviation cutting travelling times dramatically and the slowing down of migration to the New World. In the first half of the twentieth century, shipping lines had made most of their profits not from the wealthy first class traveller, but from the steerage passengers who were emigrating, principally to North America. This decline was effectively to end transatlantic passenger shipping, though the cruise market would subsequently enjoy an expansion. The most important of the British shipping lines, Cunard, would continue to use the pre-war *Queen Mary* and *Queen Elizabeth* ocean-going liners as their principal vessels until the 1960s. A state-of-the-art vessel, the *Queen Elizabeth 2* (*QE2*) was built to replace them, but it would end its days as a cruise ship. In 2003 the current Cunard flagship, the *Queen Mary 2*, was completed in French shipyards as a cruise ship but Cunard is now under part-foreign ownership. These developments did not mean an end to merchant shipping and the docks per se, merely that increasingly the shipping would be both foreign owned and constructed, and the British docks would exist largely to import manufactures from overseas.

In the post-war years there was a revolution in the commercial docks industry. In the 1940s and 1950s the docks in London, Liverpool and other commercial centres were still highly labour intensive with many, largely casual, labourers loading and unloading merchant ships. The development of containerisation meant that there was a massive decline in employment in the docks, and the advent of larger ships to transport these containers meant that the traditional London and Liverpool docks would close and be replaced by container ports closer to the open sea. These former docks were transformed after years of dereliction, particularly in London and also in Liverpool, with enormous residential and office developments.

Conclusion

Transport policy has not been a priority for many governments and is fraught with difficulty, partly because of the competing rail and road lobbies and partly because the very densely populated south-east of England ensures congestion. But the transport structure has changed fundamentally since 1945; this is a consequence partly of technological change, partly of growth in population size, but more than anything else because of the increase in real per capita incomes since the Second World War which have made travel more affordable.

11

Industrial policies and industrial relations

Introduction

There has been a fundamental transformation both in the industrial structure of Britain and in industrial relations since 1945. Britain had a highly unionised manufacturing-based economy, which has transformed into a service sector-based economy with less union activity. This has come about partly due to policy but partly due to free-market-driven changes.

In the 1930s the economic environment was largely laissez-faire, but this changed fundamentally during the Second World War when the British government undertook a very high degree of intervention in the domestic economy, directing labour and private business for the war effort. Given Britain's victory in the war, this was interpreted by a broad spectrum of society as being a successful strategy, so the public were ready to see a high degree of government intervention in the economy afterwards.

After the 1945 Labour landslide victory in the general election, the government, which was the most socialist in British history, embarked upon a programme of the nationalisation of strategic industries. Clause 4 of the constitution of the Labour Party committed it to the nationalisation of the commanding heights of the British economy, in other words, the public ownership of all large companies in Britain. The immediate post-war government did not in the event undertake such a radical programme, but it did nationalise the gas and electricity supply industries (both of which were already partly municipally owned), as well as the railways, the coal, iron and steel industries, the docks and long distance road freight haulage. However, much of British industry continued to function in a laissez-faire environment. The post-war consensus between 1945 and 1979 maintained this mixed economy, although the Conservatives did denationalise the steel industry and road freight haulage in the 1950s.

Before the First World War, the Liberal government of Sir Henry Campbell-Bannerman (1905–8) introduced the Trades Disputes Act 1906, which put the trade union movement on a modern legal basis. This resulted in an increase in union activity. After the Second World War the Attlee government strengthened the position of trade unions further. The heavy industries of coal, iron and steel, shipbuilding, car manufacture and heavy engineering had been increasingly unionised prior to the war. They had developed what the American theorist Mancur Olson referred to as 'inertial forces'. Both management and unions had long acquired certain management strategies and work practices which they were reluctant to change – hence the property of inertia. This resulted in an unwillingness to adopt new technology and work practices. The unions were particularly concerned about the unemployment they expected to result from the use of labour-saving machinery; they were also anxious to maintain demarcation between different trades in an industry, and the pay differentials associated with these demarcations. Further, the 'isolated mass thesis' tells us that because many of these industries are located in specific geographical areas where the microeconomy is dominated by just the one industry, strikes are likely to be protracted as the union members are given support by families and friends, all of whom have a vested interest in furtherance of the union aims. The notions of inertial forces and isolated mass constitute an explanation as to why British industry was slow to adapt and so went into relative decline vis-à-vis the USA, West Germany etc.

Although management may be accused of being slow to adopt new technology and work practices, the unions were particularly resistant. The adoption of labour-saving machinery bids up the marginal productivity of labour, so increasing pay, and although it destroys some jobs, it creates others. In order to reorganise labour to become more efficient, this inevitably means that labour needs to be capable of undertaking a number of tasks, and this flexibility breaks down demarcations and pay differentials. Trade unions were resistant to such changes.

An important part of the post-war consensus was a tripartite relationship between government, business and trades unions which became known as 'corporatism'. Government would invite business representatives, in the form of the Confederation of British Industry (CBI), and trade unions, in the form of the Trades Union Congress (TUC), to settle important economic matters through formal negotiation and agreement with the government.

In 1962 the Conservative government under Harold Macmillan set up the

National Economic Development Council (NEDC). This body employed the corporatist approach in an attempt to raise national economic growth from 2.7 per cent per annum to 4 per cent. It remained an advisory planning body and had little effect upon growth, but it did establish the notion of state planning of industry.

Some theorists argue that the successful development of the Far Eastern economies has been due to strategic investment in industries for long-term economic development. In Japan the Ministry of International Trade and Investment (MITI) plays an important role in long-term investment decisions. This notion of state involvement in industrial planning had its counterpart in Britain, but with modest benefits.

If we compare Britain with (West) Germany for example, particularly with regard to manufacturing industry, we see that the latter's superior productivity performance throughout much of the post-war period was caused by Germany's greater endowment of skilled labour. Although Britain enjoyed a similar proportion of workers with high skill levels to that of Germany and other major industrial countries, Britain endured a skill deficiency at the semi-skilled and lower skilled levels: only just over a quarter of the British workforce during this period possessed these skills, yet over half of the German manufacturing workforce possessed them. Also, there was a much higher proportion of unskilled workers in British industry than was the case in Germany or indeed in many other industrialised countries. So it was at the craft skill level where the productivity deficiency occurred. Investment in productivity skills creates a more flexible workforce capable of more rapid adaptation to new technology and changes in production processes, and thus determines economic growth rates.

Harold Wilson's Labour government was elected in 1964 principally on the basis that, in Wilson's words, it would transform the British economy in the 'white heat' of the technological revolution. This was intended to address Britain's productivity deficit by employing state of the art technology in industry. The government introduced the Department of Economic Affairs, with George Brown as Secretary of State, which was intended to implement a National Plan for directing industry. This plan, published in 1965, established the National Prices and Incomes Board, which was responsible for creating 'prices and incomes' policies (strictly prices and wages) to address the increasing inflationary problem created in part by the wage–price spiral (see Chapter 5). Trade unions would agree to undertake wage restraint in return for similar restraint on output prices by employers. Certain investment levels would also be agreed. These policies inevitably broke down quickly and had to be renewed. They did not address the basic productivity issue of competitiveness and so were not successful.

It was government intervention in the economy which was intended to improve national competitiveness and stimulate economic growth. The Wilson government sponsored a significant reorganisation of private industry through the Industrial Reorganisation Corporation. Mergers were promoted in the private sector by government in a number of industries, most notably the motor industry, when British Leyland was created out of the merger of much of the indigenous British car industry. These mergers were intended to improve the international competitivenes of British industries through creating economies of scale. Growth targets were set for each industry to ensure that an overall 4 per cent growth rate in the economy was achieved. Investment was to come from the private sector.

A balance-of-payments crisis in 1966 caused sterling to be sold on the foreign exchange markets, and to avoid devaluation in the Bretton Woods fixed exchange rate system (see Chapter 5) the government abandoned the National Plan, reduced public expenditure and imposed a six-month pay freeze. But during 1966 unemployment rose from 250,000 to 600,000.

Trade union militancy increased in the post-war years, particularly in the 1960s and 1970s. The number of stoppages and their duration increased, in some cases substantially, over this period. During this time a paradigm shift was taking place in the structure of British industry: Britain's productivity deficit was causing greater import penetration and so the old heavy industries were in structural decline, as such products could be more efficiently built with the lower labour costs of Far East producers. Instead the British economy saw a substantial growth in the tertiary or service sector. This sector employed a higher proportion of women and part-time workers, who tended to be less unionised and less militant than the workers in the heavy industries, and also tended to be less subject to inertial forces. Investment began to flow into these industries and away from the heavy industries.

In 1971, Edward Heath's Conservative government attempted to introduce a more free-market orientation to policy and so scrapped both the National Plan and the corporatist system, though the NEDC was retained. Unemployment rose to over one million and in consequence the government did a U-turn the following year, returning to the corporatist policies of the 1960s. This brief, though unsuccessful, dalliance with free-market economics was to prove crucial in its influence on one of Heath's Cabinet ministers,

Margaret Thatcher. When Prime Minister, Thatcher scrapped corporatism, and shifted the onus to business managers to push through change.

Through the 1960s, although the incidence of trade union disputes rose, which constitutes part of the explanation for Britain's relative economic decline, there were no major national disputes with the political significance of the 1926 General Strike. However, this changed in the 1970s. Heath's government attempted to introduce a corpus of far-reaching trade union legislation in 1971 to restrict union activity and so encourage structural change to improve productive efficiency. This brought on a significant response from the trade union movement, which boycotted the legislation, particularly so the coal miners, who enjoyed great influence by virtue of being heavily unionised; more importantly, the majority of electricity in Britain was generated by British-produced coal. A miners' strike in 1973–4 precipitated what became known as the three-day week, referring to the government's request to industry to operate, owing to reduced electricity generation, for only three of the usual five days of a working week. A general election was then called, which resulted in the defeat of the Conservatives; they were replaced by a Labour government again under the leadership of Harold Wilson, which abandoned the legislation.

In 1975 the Labour government set up the National Enterprise Board (NEB). It was intended to select businesses which appeared to have potential for growth but lacked finance from the stock exchange or the banks. The NEB would provide the businesses with grants and subsidised loans, and would purchase shares in them. Only a few small to medium-sized enterprises benefited, but the significant question was whether they truly had a future if they were unable to attract finance through commercial channels. The NEB had limited effect on the economy and was later scrapped by the Thatcher government.

The next major political strike came in the winter of 1978–9 during James Callaghan's Labour government – the so-called 'winter of discontent'. This was the nearest Britain came to the General Strike of 1926, as a substantial number of trade unions in various industries went on strike. The cause of this collective action was the stagflating economy causing a loss of jobs and a reduction in the real pay of workers. This action was largely instrumental in Labour's defeat at the 1979 general election, when Thatcher came to power.

Throughout the 1960s and 1970s nationalised industries such as the railways, coal, steel, shipbuilding and the docks were in structural decline, and governments, whether Labour or Conservative, provided substantial subsidy to keep them in business. This was partly to prevent an adverse electoral response and trade union action which might result from their more precipitous decline, and also to slow down the problem of regional unemployment. These industries in structural decline tended to be located in specific geographical areas, and despite the government support some job losses inevitably occurred. The privately owned manufacturing sector was also in structural decline throughout the post-war period, which further contributed to regional unemployment. To try and ameliorate this situation, the government would direct other industries which did wish to expand to locate in such areas. This direction of industry was known as regional policy and was practised through the 1960s and 1970s. This had indifferent results as industries were obliged to locate in areas which lacked a pool of labour with the necessary skill sets and where the chains of communication were often quite long between the administrative centre, the plants and the component suppliers.

The Thatcher government scrapped regional policy. This was consistent with Thatcher's emphasis on the free market, for it left business location decisions to managers on the basis of business criteria alone. Regarding the issue of regional unemployment, the Thatcher government encouraged occupational mobility through creating retraining schemes for those unemployed from industries in structural decline. The policy required the unemployed to move to areas where the jobs were, rather than the jobs to where the unemployed were. However, the government did little to help the geographical mobility of labour.

The London Stock Exchange continued to be the second largest in the world (after New York), and to provide private capital to British manufacturing industry. There was substantial net property income from British assets held abroad prior to the Second World War, though much of this was lost as the result of the repayment of loans to the USA. The Stock Exchange in London is accused of taking a short-term stance on investment decisions; if the return on shares in a given sector is low, there is a rapid shift of finance to other sectors where the short-term return on capital is higher. This has been a feature of the exchange throughout the post-war years, but it is also a feature of the American stock market in New York, the richest country in the world.

With respect to nationalised industries, the Wilson government renationalised the iron and steel industry in the 1960s. In 1971, the one British aero engine builder, Rolls-Royce, was nationalised by the Heath government, not for ideological reasons, but to prevent its bankruptcy. The British Leyland car company was nationalised in 1975 by the Wilson government, again, not for ideological reasons as might be imagined, but like Rolls-Royce, to prevent its bankruptcy. The British aircraft industry (airframe manufacture) and the shipbuilding industry were each merged into single organisations and nationalised – as British Aerospace and British Shipbuilders respectively – by the Callaghan government in the late 1970s, largely for ideological reasons, but it was also hoped that consolidation might enable them to compete more effectively internationally.

When Thatcher came to power in 1979 there was an ideological paradigm shift. Laissez-faire economics was the ascendant paradigm and nationalised industries were thus privatised on a substantial scale. The principal economic rationale was that the decentralised system achieves an efficient allocation of resources (Pareto optimality), therefore the privatised industries should become more efficient if subject to market forces and no longer in receipt of substantial government subsidy.

By creating a more free-market environment, the Thatcher governments would encourage a market-driven shift from an economy based on manufacturing and the extractive industries to one based on the service sector. This transition had been occurring for some time as rates of return were higher in the services than in most manufacturing, but regional policy and nationalisation had slowed down this transition.

After the Second World War manufacturing constituted more than a third of the entire economy; by the early twenty-first century it constituted less than 17 per cent, with employment falling from more than eight million to approximately four million across the same period. Of all of the services which came in to replace it, business services, finance and property grew the most, from approximately three per cent after the war to over a quarter of the entire economy today.

The Thatcher government wanted to encourage a paradigm shift in public attitudes towards the capitalist system, and it wanted to create a society which had a vested interest in maintaining this system. The great eighteenth-century free-market economist Adam Smith had commented that people were inherently self-interested and so the Thatcher government attempted to create a share-owning democracy whereby British people would have a pecuniary interest (share dividends) in the capitalist system. This was initiated by the privatisation of the utilities: gas, electricity, water and telephones. These were natural monopolies and thus subject to supernormal profits. Shares to private investors were sold at less than their anticipated market value in order to encourage sales. They were sold in small quantities to prevent the institutional shareholders from purchasing them. It was hoped that the dividends generated for shareholders by such monopolies would create a general culture of share ownership, not just in the privatised industries. This was not successful. It is true that many members of the public purchased shares in privatised utilities, but the hoped-for culture of general share ownership was not achieved.

Thatcher had been a minister in Heath's government of the early 1970s and had learnt the lesson of that government's failure to implement its trade union legislation. What Thatcher realised was that Heath had attempted to implement too many pieces of anti-union legislation simultaneously; this had given trade unionists the incentive to revolt on a large scale. Thus the Thatcher government implemented a step-by-step approach. This meant that a series of pieces of anti-union legislation would be implemented gradually over a long period. The reason for this was to ensure that there was no incentive for mass union action to prevent their introduction. For example, the government outlawed secondary picketing; now few trade unionists wanted to strike and risk their livelihoods to oppose such a narrowly confined piece of legislation. Perhaps the most significant legislation was the introduction of compulsory secret ballots for strike action. This restricted the power of the shop stewards, the local organisers of trade unionists in each firm. The shop stewards had been seen to be growing in militancy through the 1960s, and the Thatcher government believed that the practice of shop stewards asking for a show of hands of the members to instigate a strike tended to intimidate members into voting the way the stewards wanted. Legislation also required the election of union officers so they more accurately reflect the views of the membership and the abolition of 'closed shops'. The latter had been agreements between management and a union to the effect that all shop floor employees were obliged to join that union. This gave enormous monopoly power to the union, and its banning was intended to reduce this and to give workers the liberty of joining or not joining a union.

Most of the legislation in the nineteenth and early twentieth centuries which enabled unions to function at all was legislation which gave them immunity from prosecution by employers. This immunity was eroded by the Thatcher government, which gave employers powers to take legal action against unions if, for example, they did not conduct a secret ballot, or undertook secondary picketing. It also banned strikes in the intelligence organisation the Government Communications Headquarters (GCHQ) for national security reasons, rather crassly giving each employee £1,000 in compensation.

Despite the attempts by the Thatcher government to prevent a strike being precipitated by the introduction of anti-trade union legislation, this indeed was to occur. The National Union of Mineworkers (NUM), which had been largely responsible for the Conservatives losing the 1974 general election and the ushering in of a Labour government, would try and do the same thing again in 1984, under its new and militant general secretary, Arthur Scargill. The government knew such a strike was brewing and ensured that large stocks of coal were available at the pit heads and the power stations. It helped precipitate the strike in the spring, when the days were getting warmer and longer so that there would be less demand for electricity. Although the government used the police to help break the strike for those miners who wanted to return to work, and also used the police to guard imported coal from the ports, the strike nevertheless was to last a year. In spring 1985 the union realised it had lost, and a return to work became inevitable. The Thatcher government then accelerated the pit closure programme to prevent such a strike occurring again, and the NUM, the shock troops of the trade union movement, was neutralised.

Since the 1980s there has been an intellectual debate over whether there are changes in geopolitical and international economic relations which are qualitatively new phenomena. Theorists subscribing to the qualitative change model tend to fall into one of two camps: they believe either in the notion of 'globalisation', or in another distinct notion, that of 'regionalisation'. Those who believe that no such qualitative change is taking place interpret what is happening as the notion of 'internationalisation'.

Internationalisation is the notion that there is nothing qualitatively different in the geopolitical and international economic relationships between nation states in the contemporary world by comparison with what occurred, say, in the nineteenth century. Internationalisationalists argue that the only distinction is a quantitative one, that nations have been interconnected by an increasing volume of international trade and capital movements. Regionalisationalists argue that there has indeed been a qualitative change in these relationships, but that this change has the character of the world breaking up into regional trading blocs, or customs unions: the European Union, the North American Free Trade Agreement, the Association of Southeast Asian Nations, Asia-Pacific Economic Cooperation, etc. Thus these relationships are to be characterised as increased trade and capital flows within each trading block, while political constraints restrict trade and capital flows between these regional organisations.

Globalisation has at least two possible interpretations. Some theorists argue that it constitutes a qualitative change of the relationship between the governments of nation states and the board rooms of multinational corporations (MNCs). They argue that the growth of MNCs since the Second World War has resulted in some having a turnover greater than the GDP of many smaller industrial countries. This gives MNCs considerable bargaining power with the governments of nation states, and allows them to enjoy the largest single influence over the policy agenda of those governments.

Other theorists argue that globalisation is indeed occurring but argue from the perspective of a 'long-wave' or 'stage' theory of capitalism. This theory refers to the expansionary and contractionary phases or 'waves' to which capitalist history has been subject for generations. It predicts that this wave motion is changing such that growth is becoming more consistent and stable because of a complex network of supra-national institutions, accepted norms and government laws and regulations. Institutions such as the International Monetary Fund and the World Trade Organization and more effective national legislation are creating a more effective framework for the expansion of MNCs. Thus globalisation is the process of creating these structures, and by so doing the expansionary phase of capitalism becomes more stable and more protracted, and periods of stagnation become shorter and less severe.

It is not clear as yet as to whether the latter interpretation is correct, and it would be inappropriate to suggest that the long period of continuous economic growth which Britain has experienced in the 1990s and the early twenty-first century is the result of this process, as much of western Europe has not enjoyed it. But the former interpretation is significant; the British government has been influenced significantly by MNCs in its industrial policy, particularly in respect of foreign direct investment (FDI). FDI is the notion of an MNC creating a subsidiary in another country, or purchasing such a subsidiary from another owner. It is one of the major causal factors in international economic growth.

The proactivity of governments in attracting FDI has become an increasingly important phenomenon. Governments benefit through job creation, reduced unemployment payments, increased tax yield, import substitution, increased foreign currency reserves and balance of trade enhancement. Thus they compete with one another to attract FDI, offering lucrative financial incentives to encourage the MNC to undertake FDI in their country rather than that of a trading competitor.

In the 1980s the Thatcher government's new classical macroeconomic policies and industrial polices of removing subsidies from nationalised industries and privatising them meant a substantial rise in unemployment to around three million, the highest since the Depression of the 1930s. The government sought to address this problem through stimulating inward FDI. This was the policy of attracting mainly American and Japanese high technology businesses in sectors of the economy where indigenous British businesses were either not present or poorly represented. It was also a policy of ensuring that Britain was increasingly integrated into the global capitalist system, and reliant upon businesses from other capitalist countries. The purpose of this was to ensure that no future Labour government could reverse Margaret Thatcher's free-market reforms.

By the end of the twentieth century Britain had accumulated £252.4bn ($400bn) of FDI, of which nearly half originated from the US. Japanese FDI had been relatively small, although by the end of the century approximately 8 per cent of FDI was sourced from Japan. Britain enjoys more inward FDI than any other country with the exception of the USA, with more than a third of its manufacturing sector now being foreign owned. Britain is also one of the largest exporters of FDI, mostly to the USA, Europe and the Far East. In the late 1990s and early twenty-first century there has been a wave of service sector FDI, most particularly in telecommunications and financial services.

FDI into the EU has become increasingly important particularly for Far Eastern and American companies, who wish to exploit the large EU internal market but circumvent the tariff and quota restrictions to which they would be subject if they exported to the EU. Of all inward FDI into the EU, Britain has attracted around 25 per cent. Of particular concern to the location of FDI in the EU are the issues of the single currency, the euro, and the social legislation (on pay and working conditions). Britain is outside the euro, and attempts by Britain to attract FDI are hampered by the fact that any MNC producing goods in Britain and exporting to the rest of the EU is subject to an adverse exchange rate. Locating FDI in the euro zone has the advantage of reducing currency exchange costs and exchange rate uncertainty. However, Britain has a more flexible labour market with less social legislation, and so business costs in Britain are less than those of continental Europe. Yet, when the euro was introduced, FDI in the zone rose by 11 per cent, while for EU countries outside the zone it fell by 18 per cent. In consequence Britain has been losing FDI to Spain, Ireland and the Netherlands and larger EU economies have also enjoyed an increase. However, the big new development is FDI flooding into the eastern European countries which were inducted into the EU in May 2004, with their low labour costs and modest regulatory framework, many of which will become part of the euro zone in due course.

The location of FDI is based on the access to markets, the availability of a skilled workforce, good transport links and also cultural amenities. Thus much of British FDI in manufacturing is located in the south-east of England, near continental European markets. The north-east of England, Scotland and Wales have been obliged to spend significant sums of taxpayers' money to attract FDI, and much of this has been in the market sectors of cars and electronics. Wales has an above-average proportion of foreign FDI, and northern Scotland has substantial FDI in North Sea oil production.

The Japanese companies tended to build factories on green field sites and employ staff who had not been employed in that industry before. This may seem odd, for example, for a new car plant, as it may seem natural to locate it in an area where cars have been traditionally built; that way you have a skilled workforce in the area, component suppliers, and ancillary workers. However, you also have inertial forces. Setting up a company on a green field site with a workforce fresh to the industry means that the workforce can be taught to employ the modern working practices of the company with little or no resistance.

Foreign-owned firms tend to be more productive, pay more, be more capital intensive and use more advanced technology than British firms. However, there are relatively few 'spill over' effects that create productivity improvements in domestic firms – a potential benefit normally quoted by the government to justify its high level of grants to attract FDI. Those less competitive British businesses are subject to significant attrition from foreign MNCs, but British businesses with a well-developed technological base benefit by the increased competition from FDI.

It was technically difficult to introduce competition to the utilities, because they are, *ex hypothesi*, natural monopolies. British Telecom (BT) had a small competitor introduced at privatisation, called Mercury (later owned by Cable and Wireless), but because it had to transmit its services on BT lines, BT was able to increase the standing charge to customers yet reduce its call prices to compete with Mercury. The electricity-generating system was broken up into a duopoly of coal-fired producers called National Power and PowerGen, plus a company for the nuclear generators, and, because of the threat from the

NUM, a programme of gas-fired power stations was initiated. But the distribution system was still a natural monopoly and, although it was broken up into regional electricity companies (RECs), the monopoly issue remained. Subsequently some additional competition has been introduced in the utilities in the form of sales and marketing, where, for example, gas companies can sell electricity.

The privatised utilities required regulation to prevent them exploiting their monopoly power by substantially increasing prices to customers. The system of regulation set up by the Conservatives was a series of quangos or 'offices', such as Oftel, the office of telecommunications for the telephone industry, now renamed Ofcom and concerned with communications more generally. Such regulators have statutory powers to enable them to intervene in pricing decisions. They have to balance the requirement of low prices to consumers against the need for investment in the industry.

The Thatcher government also proceeded to privatise British Petroleum, British Steel, British Aerospace, British Airways, British Shipbuilders and Rolls-Royce amongst others. Indeed, by the time Thatcher was replaced by John Major in 1990, all the principal industries which had been nationalised were back in private hands, with only the exception of British Rail, which was privatised by the Major government (see Chapter 10). The Post Office remains a nationalised industry, having originally been a government department prior to nationalisation.

Since the Second World War, agriculture had been administered by the Ministry of Agriculture, Fisheries and Food, but the New Labour government of Tony Blair combined agriculture with environmental issues to create the Department for Environment, Food and Rural Affairs. Approximately three-quarters of the total land area of Britain is farmland. Immediately after the war the agricultural industry constituted around 5 per cent of the value of GDP, and employed one and a quarter million people. By the beginning of the twenty-first century this had fallen to around 1 per cent of GDP and employment to less than a third of a million, though it had been more than 400,000 only a decade before. There are approximately 300,000 farms in Britain at an average size of 100 hectares (250 acres) in Scotland, 50 hectares in England and 40 in Wales. This is considerably larger than the average European farm size of approximately 20 hectares; however, the number of employees per hectare is much lower in Britain than the European average, thus British agriculture tends to be much more efficient than elsewhere in Europe.

In the 1960s and again in the 1990s dairy farms suffered two separate bouts of foot and mouth disease, not a terminal disorder, but one which required the slaughter of many cattle to prevent infection spreading. Also in the 1990s cattle were struck by the lethal brain disorder bovine spongiform encephalopathy (BSE), which can be transmitted to humans as Creutzfeldt–Jakob disease (CJD). The EU stopped cattle exports from Britain for a period as a result.

Britain imports most of its agricultural produce and also the majority of its fish, to the value of some £1.5 billion of fish in 2005. The British fishing fleet landed fish worth over £500 million at the same time; it also exports those species of fish and fish products for which customer tastes are stronger abroad, which in some cases are landed directly in foreign markets by British fishing vessels. In 2005 Britain's fish-processing industry employed more than 18,000 people.

When Britain joined the European Economic Community in 1973, its agriculture received subsidies under the Common Agricultural Policy (CAP; see Chapter 14). Despite the fact the British agricultural output had been growing, the CAP subsidies failed to keep pace with inflation and in consequence agriculture contracted. In the ten years after joining, the number of dairy farms fell by half, cereal farms by nearly a third and overall employment by a quarter. When sterling was ejected from the European Monetary System in 1992 and fell in value (see Chapter 5), exports rose including agricultural exports, increasing farm incomes. However, since the subsequent recovery of the British economy and growth in the value of sterling, exports have fallen, as have farm incomes. This is part of a long-term trend, as farm incomes have fallen consistently since the Second World War. As CAP subsidies are reduced farm incomes will fall further.

In 1992 Major's Conservative government negotiated an opt-out for Britain from the Social Chapter of the Maastricht treaty, which committed all EU governments to introduce a national minimum wage (NMW). Major did this because his government was about to abolish the trade boards or wage councils which Winston Churchill had introduced in 1909, in his first government job as President of the Board of Trade in the Liberal government of Herbert Asquith. These boards or councils created minimum wages for the major industries. This was not an NMW, as not all industries were covered, and different industries had different minimum wages, but nevertheless, wages and therefore prices were not fully flexible in accordance with the free-market model. Another reason for abolishing the boards was that the industries covered by the 1909 Act had diminished greatly in size by the 1990s and were thus only of limited importance to the economy. The boards had been weakened in 1986 and were finally abolished in 1993.

However, the New Labour government of Tony Blair decided to opt in to the Social Chapter in 1998 and so the NMW was introduced the following year, the Low Pay Commission having been set up to administer it. The wage was set at a level which would not create appreciable unemployment (initially it only affected 4.5 per cent of the labour force). The motivation for introducing this measure was to placate the left-wing members of the Labour Party without appreciably undermining business competitiveness, but it did shift some of the cost of supporting low income families from the social security budget to businesses. There is one area of the economy where an NMW can create employment: this is where labour is demanded monopsonistically (by a single employer). In such a situation the market power of the monopsonist is such that it forces the wage rate and the level of employment below what would be the case in a competitive market. An NMW forces the employer to pay closer to the competitive wage and so more labour is attracted into the organisation at the higher wage rate. The irony of this is that the really big monopsony employers are government departments, such as the Ministry of Defence, and departments employing ancillary workers such as hospital cleaners or school dinner ladies. Thus the NMW is forcing government to pay more to many of its own low-paid employees!

The Major government introduced the 1993 Trade Union Reform Act, which gave individuals the freedom to join any union they liked, thus eroding the monopoly power of individual unions, and required that unions give seven days' notice prior to a strike. The Blair government adopted the Conservative legislation, which constrained the activities of trade unions with regard to postal ballots, the abolition of closed shops and secondary picketing, the election of union officers etc. In fact it extended the requirement of unions to give notice prior to a strike to fourteen days.

The Blair government also inducted a sizeable number of businesspeople into government as ministers, advisers and heads of task forces, whereas only about 2 per cent of these functions would be undertaken by trades unionists. However, it also sought to depoliticise government actions by a limited return to 'corporatism', through seeking prior agreements between the TUC and the CBI. Meanwhile, the Bank of England's Monetary Policy Committee, introduced by the Blair government (see Chapter 5), absolved the government of the responsibility for managing inflationary wage settlements, as such settlements now led to a rise in interest rates to choke off their inflationary effects.

The EU Working Time Directive, which is intended to restrict working hours, was implemented in Britain only in a limited way, permitting some flexibility to undertake overtime work beyond the prescribed hours. The Blair government introduced the 'Fairness at Work' measure, which has modified the Conservative legislation a little: it gives statutory rights to union recognition, but there remain derecognition ballots (where the workforce can vote to derecognise a union), and there is very limited government regulation. The measure has reduced the unfair dismissal qualifying period from two years to one, and there has been an extension of maternity leave to eighteen weeks. GCHQ employees were given back their union rights after a no-strike agreement was negotiated. The net result of these measures was to retain much of the labour market flexibility of the Thatcher and Major eras, but to shift policy marginally in favour of the European 'social model'.

The New Labour government has made no attempt to renationalise industries. Indeed, shortly after election in 1997 they extended privatisation to the air traffic control system. However, although the Labour Party has relinquished the notion of the ownership of assets in order to control the allocation of resources, it has replaced it by one of regulation. The degree to which the government has regulated the private sector has been very substantial indeed.

The policy of using private companies to provide major public projects is a phenomenon which was initiated by the Conservatives in 1992 and has been developed by Labour. In this policy, known as the public–private partnership (PPP) or private finance initiative (PFI), capital projects are financed, constructed and operated by the private sector and the services provided are purchased through a contract (usually lasting thirty years) by government. Although this reduces the public liability for investment funds ab initio, the policy has been criticised on the grounds that the private sector successfully shifts risk to the public sector and wealth to the private sector, so it is more expensive for the taxpayer in the long run.

Throughout the post-war period governments sought to prevent monopolies. They did this through a body known as the Monopolies and Mergers Commission (MMC), now known as the Competition Commission. In recent years there has been a tension in national policy between the desire to keep prices low for consumers, and for companies to enjoy economies of scale, the latter requiring mergers and acquisitions. In the increasingly integrated global market, international competition is ever more important. Thus the MMC and later the Competition Commission have increasingly sanctioned mergers and acquisitions by British companies in order to enable them to compete more effectively. International competition is deemed sufficient to keep prices down.

Conclusion

British industry is more productive and more profitable as a service sector-based economy than it was when manufacturing predominated. Despite this there is much wistful pining for the old manufacturing base. This has been retained in other European countries, but usually with government policies which have caused considerable resource misallocation. The sectoral shift in the British economy has been significantly more responsible than any other single factor for the transformation in the growth of the economy. However, average national productivity levels have dropped since 2001 because of a fall in productivity in the public sector due to the massive growth in spending and employment. Thus Britain's average productivity is below that of Germany, France and the USA.

12

Foreign and defence policies

Introduction

In 1945 British armed forces had a global reach, whereas today Britain has a small defence force with limited capability and Britain's foreign policy has diminished in line with its defence capabilities. The ability to influence world affairs via foreign policy is predicated upon the size of a nation's armed forces, which is in turn predicated on the size of the national economy. Thus it is Britain's relative economic decline as well as the loss of empire which has been responsible for the decline in defence capability and the reduced significance of foreign policy.

Britain had become reliant upon the USA for its defence requirements by the Second World War. It is true that Britain had successfully denied the German Luftwaffe air superiority over southern England during the Battle of Britain in 1940, and consequently forced Nazi Germany to postpone indefinitely its plan to invade England ('Operation Sealion'). Britain achieved this utilising largely its own resources, but it was abundantly clear nevertheless that Britain only had a fraction of the resources necessary to defeat Germany. When Japan entered the war it started to annex British colonies in the Far East in rapid succession. Only the entry of the USSR and the US into the war enabled Britain to achieve ultimate victory. With the post-war threat from the USSR it was equally clear that Britain would require defence assistance from the US, just as it had during the war, and this meant that British foreign policy was also to be profoundly influenced by the US. Britain's 'special relationship' with the US (a term coined by Winston Churchill) has remained policy to the present day.

This recognition of the USA's supremacy in leading the defence of Western interests led the British government, and particularly Clement Attlee's Foreign Secretary, Ernest Bevin, to be foremost in supporting the creation of the

North Atlantic Treaty Organisation (NATO) in 1949. This provided an American-led defence of western Europe. But at this time, Britain still believed that it had discretion to act independently in respect of those foreign and defence policy issues which related purely to its own sphere of influence and which were outside NATO. The first significant episode of post-war cooperation with the USA on defence matters occurred when Britain deployed forces in Korea in 1950 to fight alongside the Americans in the three-year war against communist forces supported by China and the USSR, which ended in stalemate.

When the western Europeans asked Britain to join a European defence organisation, the European Defence Community, in the early 1950s, Britain declined, and the organisation collapsed shortly afterwards. The Western European Union was developed to replace it, but this remained moribund for many years, only being revived in the 1990s as the European Union's embryonic defence body. Britain's position was summed up by Churchill when he remarked that Britain would always choose the US rather than Europe.

Britain's post-war defence policy was defined by its NATO commitment, and this in turn was predicated upon American foreign policy: the 'Truman doctrine', the containment of Soviet-sponsored communist expansionism. To this end, Britain supplied an army contingent to NATO in West Germany, the British Army of the Rhine (BAOR). This was the first time in history that Britain had a standing army in another European country. Britain also supplied a contingent of the RAF to West Germany. Britain's naval responsibility was to guard the Atlantic approaches against both the Soviet surface fleet and, more significantly, its submarines. Britain also facilitated American military bases and early-warning equipment on British soil. To sum up, British policy was therefore to participate in West German defence (army and air force), to engage predominantly in anti-submarine warfare (navy) and to conduct domestic air defence (air force).

Churchill, when he returned to office in 1951, attempted to resume the very high degree of influence on American defence and foreign policy which Britain had had during the war, but the economic supremacy of the USA meant that they had very limited interest in this. This fact had already been appreciated by Bevin, who had prompted Attlee to go ahead with the development of a British atomic bomb partly as a way of influencing American policy decisions. When Churchill returned to power he was surprised at how advanced this project was. Codenamed 'Hurricane', it was being built at

Aldermaston in Berkshire and was first tested in 1952. Three state-of-the-art British jet bombers were designed to carry it, the Vickers Valiant, the Handley-Page Victor and the Avro Vulcan, which collectively became known as the V-bomber force. The Valiants subsequently suffered from metal fatigue and were withdrawn from service in the 1960s, while the Victors were subsequently converted to flight refuelling tankers, leaving only the Vulcans as constituting the V-bomber force. However, by this time, as recounted below, the strategic deterrent would pass to the Royal Navy and the Vulcans were relegated to a conventional (non-nuclear) role.

In 1957 Britain tested its first hydrogen bomb (code name 'Grapple') and thus entered the thermonuclear age, with the V-bomber force carrying the bomb in service. This development was used as leverage to negotiate a close nuclear agreement with the USA, ironically ending Britain's independence in this regard as it has subsequently used a US-designed bomb.

The defence dependency on the USA meant a concomitant increasing foreign policy dependency. Initially after the Second World War, Britain attempted to restore the status quo ante in its foreign, and particularly its colonial, policy, using its post-war loan from the USA (see Chapter 5), not to concentrate on rebuilding its industrial infrastructure but rather to finance its 'blue water' navy which policed the Empire. Perhaps surprisingly, this was a policy of Attlee's Labour government. This policy was looked upon with some disdain by the USA, which opposed colonialism in principle, but the Truman doctrine meant that American foreign policy was to maintain stability within its hegemonic fiefdom, and British colonial policy was to some extent consistent with this objective.

Legitimate aspirations for independence by Britain's colonial possessions caused a splintering away of the Empire in post-war years, most notably with the independence of India in 1947. But this was not yet a consequence of British policy but rather a consequence of political agitation by indigenous elements within the colonial possessions.

When Churchill was forced into retirement by his party in 1955 he was replaced by Anthony Eden, who had been Foreign Secretary on and off since the 1930s. When the President of Egypt, Gamal Abdul Nasser, nationalised the Suez Canal, Eden interpreted this as a direct threat to Britain's long-established lines of communication to its Empire in the east, and portrayed Nasser as another Hitler. A vast armada was organised with the French (who had controlled the canal with Britain since the nineteenth century) and, with a little help from Israel, the canal was returned to Franco-British stewardship.

The US President, Dwight Eisenhower, had hardly been consulted in this endeavour and promptly went through the roof, threatening to collapse the value of sterling on the foreign exchange markets if Britain did not withdraw. The USA was uninterested in Britain's imperial lines of communication but was most concerned with the response of the USSR to these events, and was not prepared to risk the possibility of Soviet forces moving into the region on the pretext of a request for help by Egypt. Britain consequently withdrew from the canal and Eden resigned in January 1957 on the pretext of ill health.

Early in the twentieth century the USA had clearly overtaken Britain as the pre-eminent economic power, but had voluntarily retreated into 'splendid isolation' in the inter-war years and thus had not projected strategic power commensurate with the magnitude of its economic strength. As a consequence Britain had filled the power vacuum and thus had been subject to an 'illusion of grandeur'. What the Suez crisis did was to dispel that illusion, and ever since Britain has been obliged to 'consult' the USA on all substantive foreign and defence policy issues.

The loss of Britain's self-perceived status as a superpower, the increasing economic liability of its largely Third World Empire and the colonies' legitimate aspirations for independence led Harold Macmillan in February 1960 to deliver his 'wind of change' speech in Cape Town, which marked a fundamental policy shift for Britain. Now it would be official British policy to facilitate the independence of its remaining colonial possessions. The policy of dismantling the Empire had begun. This policy was, however, determined more by Britain's self-interest than by an acceptance of the moral superiority of self-governance. It was an acceptance of Britain's increasing inability to hang on to these colonies, and of the fact that, on a strict cost–benefit analysis, the colonies were costing Britain more in policing and administration than they were benefiting Britain in trade and so domestic economic growth. Meanwhile, the term 'Empire' was increasingly being replaced by the more benign term 'Commonwealth', and now former colonial possessions were invited to join the Commonwealth organisation as independent self-governing nations. This organisation, which in its present form dates from 1949, has its headquarters in London, is run by a secretary general and has Elizabeth II as its current head.

In the 1950s the Conservative government produced a defence White Paper, for which the secretary of state, Duncan Sandys, was responsible, which committed Britain to a guided-missile defence policy. The era of 'push-button' warfare had arrived. To that end the English Electric Thunderbird and

Bristol Bloodhound surface-to-air missiles (SAMs) were developed, and the English Electric Lightning became both the first and the last all-British supersonic fighter aircraft, as manned defence systems were assumed to have become obsolete. However, this policy would soon be reversed. But even on the missile programme, Britain's growing economic problems in the early 1960s led to the cancellation of the tactical nuclear missile Blue Water, which in turn was largely responsible for the closure of the English Electric missile facility which developed it. As part of the guided-missile programme a medium-range ballistic missile with a nuclear warhead was to be developed in Britain for strategic defence. A liquid-fuelled system intended to be launched from silos was produced, called Blue Streak. Cost escalation, and the acceptance that Britain's economy was incapable of sustaining such a unilateral programme, precipitated its cancellation in 1960.

The 'U2 incident' in 1960, where the American reconnaissance pilot Gary Powers was shot down flying a Lockheed U2 spy plane on a high altitude photographic sortie over the USSR, graphically illustrated for the first time how advanced Soviet high altitude SAMs had become. This at once rendered the British V-bomber force and its high altitude tactics obsolete. Two measures were introduced to combat this: firstly, the operation of a 'hi-lo-lo-hi' mission profile, whereby the bombers dropped to low altitude in the combat zone in order to fly beneath the enemy's radar; and secondly, the adoption of Blue Steel stand-off nuclear missiles (fired from aircraft while outside the enemy's defences) to be deployed by the V-bombers in place of the freefall bombs.

With the cancellation of Blue Streak, it was decided that a stand-off system with a longer range than Blue Steel was needed if Soviet defences were to be successfully penetrated. The USA was developing just such a system, called Skybolt, for the US Air Force. It was also developing a silo-based inter-continental ballistic missile (ICBM) system, to be called Minuteman, and a submarine-based ICBM system, to be called Polaris. Macmillan wanted to buy Skybolt off the shelf from the USA as this would cost the British taxpayer substantially less than developing a system in Britain. Also the V-bombers could easily be modified to carry it. There was one significant problem, however: the American contractors could not make Skybolt work success-fully. This was of peripheral importance to the Americans, as Minuteman and Polaris adequately satisfied their strategic requirements. President John F. Kennedy offered to *give* Macmillan Skybolt, but the British were unsure they could make it work if the Americans could not. Instead Macmillan was obliged to purchase the Polaris ICBM system, which meant vastly increased cost as new nuclear submarines had to be constructed to deploy it.

It was Harold Wilson's Labour government which introduced Polaris into service, having reduced the number of submarines from five to four. It was surprising that it went into service at all, with a cash-strapped government and given that the Labour Party, when previously in opposition, had advocated unilateral nuclear disarmament in a conference decision under its previous leader, Hugh Gaitskell, a decision which Gaitskell vowed to overturn. Wilson's Secretary of State for Defence, Denis Healey, was obliged to cut other defence commitments drastically because of domestic economic problems and the cost of Polaris, these cuts including the cancellation of the British Aircraft Corporation TSR-2 supersonic nuclear bomber; when its American equivalent, the General Dynamics F111, was ordered as a cheaper replacement, that was cancelled too. For the navy there was the phasing out of the large fleet aircraft carriers.

The Macmillan government had already signalled the end of Empire and with it, on cost grounds, defence deployment and foreign as well as colonial policy interests would be scaled down. This was significantly apparent east of Suez, with the removal of forces and scaling down of interests in the geographical areas of the Indian sub-continent and the Far East. Hong Kong excepted, this was accomplished in the late 1960s, though Wilson was reluctant to do it. At the same time, American President Lyndon Johnson asked the Wilson government for British participation in the Vietnam War, a request which Wilson declined on both economic and political grounds, despite supporting Johnson's policy in Vietnam overall.

As Britain's ability to go it alone on defence projects was being compromised on cost grounds, collaborative developments of military aircraft such as the SEPECAT Jaguar (with the French) and the Panavia Tornado (with the Germans and Italians) were initiated in the 1960s and 1970s respectively. However, warship production was still being conducted in Britain by British companies, as was production of the main battle tanks, the Chieftain and later the Challenger. The Belgian-designed FN assault rifle was adopted by the Army under American pressure to be consistent with other European NATO countries, and would see service throughout the 1960s, 1970s and 1980s. It was replaced by the British-designed Royal Ordnance SA 80 rifle in the 1990s, although this had to be retrospectively modified to address technical problems.

From the 1960s the Wilson Labour government envisaged an upgraded development of the warhead to the Polaris system and so initiated the Chevaline project. This project continued in secrecy through the 1970s under another Labour Prime Minster, James Callaghan, while the Labour Party rank and file continued to be largely opposed to nuclear weapons. Chevaline was finally introduced by the Conservative government of Margaret Thatcher, who then decided that the whole Polaris system required replacement, and again the lowest-cost option was to adopt an American system. A system called Trident C4 was then being developed and Thatcher wanted it. However, in the USA, the administration of President Ronald Reagan wanted to deploy a more powerful system, Trident D5, and so Britain was obliged to purchase this at higher cost, and was also obliged to pay some of the development costs.

With the purchase of Polaris and then Trident from the USA it was assumed that this would cement Anglo-American cooperation in the special relationship. But the hegemonic superiority of the USA meant that Britain could only exert very limited influence. The Thatcher–Reagan axis was a personally convivial relationship, but the disparity of American influence was nevertheless very clear. When Argentina invaded the Falkland Islands (Malvinas) in 1982, the USA had been a supporter of both countries (Argentina was a bulwark against communist influence in South America) and reluctantly sided with Britain only because Argentina had been the aggressor. Also, the USA feared that a failure on its part so to do might indicate that other countries could act aggressively, as Argentina had.

Britain had given up its fleet carriers in the 1970s, with their slant decks and steam catapults, carrying conventional fixed-wing aircraft. This had been done on grounds of cost. All future naval activity was expected to be conducted in Britain's NATO area of operation in the North Sea, where land-based strike aircraft and maritime reconnaissance aircraft could give the fleet air cover. The Falklands war was an 'out of area' operation, and for air cover the fleet was reliant upon the small V/STOL (vertical/short take-off and landing) British Aerospace Sea Harrier, flown from aircraft carriers originally intended to deploy only helicopters. Also, these carriers had not originally been equipped with shipboard-launched airborne maritime reconnaissance aircraft. The Americans helped by supplying intelligence information from their spy satellites. The Thatcher government subsequently decided to deploy its own spy satellite, codenamed Zircon, but this project was eventually abandoned.

After the Falklands war, the Reagan administration decided to invade the small Caribbean island of Grenada to remove a communist-inspired leadership. This was done despite the fact that Grenada was a British colony and without British consent or participation. The Thatcher government was naturally aghast at this, but could do nothing. This most aptly demonstrated the severe limitations of Britain's ability to influence the USA.

In 1986, Britain's last remaining helicopter manufacturer, Westland, was in financial difficulty and the Secretary of State for Defence, Michael Heseltine, wanted to see the company rescued by a European consortium. Thatcher opposed this; she wanted to see it taken over by an American manufacturer. This appeared to many as an insignificant issue given the very small size of the Westland company, and thus the minor economic and unemployment consequences associated with its possible demise. In fact the issue was much more significant for three reasons. Firstly, Britain was still attempting to hang on to a fully integrated national defence industry in order to be able to provide a very high proportion of its defence equipment from British companies. This meant that (the strategic nuclear programme excepted), as Britain was not being supplied with very much defence equipment from other countries, it was not subject to the problem of political influence by their governments (except for the USA, of course). Helicopters are vital to modern armed forces, and Westland, as the sole British helicopter manufacturer, was thus vital to this policy. Secondly, Heseltine was in favour of further European integration, and to advance this he supported Westland's merger with a European consortium, whereas Thatcher preferred an American takeover of Westland if there had to be outside influence at all. Thirdly, Heseltine was a believer in government intervention in industrial matters, so he was ideologically opposed to Thatcher's free-market industrial policies. The Westland affair brought this difference to a head, and when Thatcher attempted to constrain Heseltine by requiring, at a Cabinet meeting, that all of his policy enunciations be cleared by her before they were released, he walked out and resigned from the government. He would challenge her for the premiership four years later (though neither would in fact win that election) and so end the Thatcher era.

The orientation of British foreign and defence policy did not change significantly after the collapse of the USSR, apart from some scaling back of forces, the increased flexibility to undertake 'out of area' operations (since the Falklands war) and the development of rapid reaction forces. The emphasis, as during the Cold War, remained on conventional and nuclear deterrents to be used in major land wars. The one significant exception was policy in Northern Ireland, where special forces and MI5 (the domestic intelligence organisation) had been involved since the late 1960s, as well as Scotland Yard's Special Branch, to deal with the IRA threat in London (see Chapter 3).

The Thatcher government had been stalwart in its support for US President George Bush Senior's policy of ejecting Iraqi forces from Kuwait after the leader of Iraq, Saddam Hussein, had annexed Kuwait in 1990. The first Gulf war ensued, by which time Thatcher had been replaced by John Major. Major provided British military support for the American-led operation, which was successful.

In Tony Blair's first period of Labour government, the Foreign Office undertook an 'ethical' foreign policy based on stricter controls of arms sales to developing countries. This continued until Blair sacked Robin Cook as Foreign Secretary, after which little was heard of this measure. Blair replaced Cook with the former Home Secretary Jack Straw, who had no policy agenda of his own, and thus Blair could exercise foreign policy directly. He went on to sack Straw in 2006 when he started to develop an agenda, and replaced him with the former environment secretary Margaret Beckett.

On 1 July 1997 the last significant piece of the British Empire, Hong Kong, was returned to China. Britain actually had acquired Hong Kong island in perpetuity, but had taken out a lease of ninety-nine years on Kowloon and the New Territories, located on the mainland, which expired on the above date. Britain decided to return all of it to China, partly because Hong Kong had been acquired under duress, but principally because of the implausibility of maintaining it as a colony against the policy of China, a vast nuclear power.

Shortly after Blair became PM he offered American President Bill Clinton unequivocal support at the time of the latter's scandalous sexual relationship with Monica Lewinsky. This was a deft move as it elicited a quid pro quo in the form of Clinton's involvement as an honest broker in the Northern Ireland peace settlement (see Chapter 3). After the election of George W. Bush to the American presidency, Blair offered him the same unequivocal support that he had offered Clinton, resulting in Bush's request for Britain to participate in the second Gulf war to execute regime change in Iraq, removing Saddam and introducing democracy. This came as a shock to the Blair government, which could hardly turn down the Americans, having offered them unequivocal support. The policy incurred considerable political costs for Blair in terms of loss of electoral support as well as strong opposition from within his own party.

The Blair government is developing two aircraft carriers to replace the three that are currently in service. It is purchasing a replacement for the Harrier strike aircraft developed mostly in the USA, and is buying the European collaborative air superiority fighter the Eurofighter, now renamed the Typhoon. It is also looking at a replacement for the Trident nuclear deterrent, despite the collapse of the USSR and the end of the Cold War.

Blair also decided that Britain should participate in some cooperative areas of EU defence and foreign policy (see Chapter 14). Although still opposed to a high degree of integration in the EU, Blair wanted to participate more fully in EU matters than the Conservatives had in order to gain leverage for reciprocal support for his own policy agenda of environmental and development issues (see Chapter 13), plus reforms of the EU (see Chapter 14).

The threat from Islam-inspired terrorism is the new principal foreign and defence policy issue. This has necessitated the refocusing of MI5 (which monitors domestic threats) and MI6 (the Secret Intelligence Service, which operates abroad), together with Scotland Yard, all in close cooperation with US agencies and those of other industrial countries. The long-run consequences of this policy are unknown.

Conclusion

Today Britain lacks the requisite qualities to be a hegemonic power. It seeks influence with the USA, but the USA, as a hegemonic power, has little interest in accepting that influence. The EU has influence of significance by dint of its sheer size; Britain could exercise some influence via the EU but just cannot decide whether to ally itself with the USA exclusively or with the EU. With the EU, and increasingly China, growing in international influence, Britain is likely to continue to lose out.

13

Environmental and overseas development policies

Introduction

Environmental and overseas development matters have long been amongst the least consequential of government policies, domestic economic and social matters having occupied much more government time. But in recent years the environment and development have been elevated in their importance as the world becomes a more integrated place.

Environment

Environmental economics concerns the consequences to the natural environment of economic activity. These consequences can be termed 'externalities', because the costs or benefits of economic activity to the environment are external to those activities themselves; in other words, they are not reflected in the cost and revenue structure of the market mechanisms for those activities. This is usually known as market failure.

An externality can be a by-product of production or consumption, giving us two categories: production and consumption externalities. For example, a chemical plant which is discharging toxic effluent damages the environment as the result of its production processes – this is a production externality; whereas improvements made by some residents to their homes enhance the utility of other homes in the street – this is a consumption externality, as the neighbours derive benefit for which they do not have to pay. The government is uninterested in consumption externalities, but production externalities are central to its environmental policy.

The problem with a production externality is that it imposes costs upon society that the polluter does not incur. Let us consider the chemical plant example: suppose the plant is polluting a river which is fished commercially.

The activity of the plant is reducing the income of the fishermen by damaging the fish stock; but the chemical plant incurs no cost for doing this if it is left to the free market. In other words, there is a divergence between the marginal private cost (the plant's costs of production as reflected in its supply curve) and the marginal social cost, which is the cost to society as a whole. The difference between these two costs is known as the marginal external cost, and this is the environmental cost of a production externality.

The British government has traditionally used regulation as the principal way of controlling these externalities, by specifying limits upon the amount of different kinds of pollution it tolerates in the environment. However, the quantity of information necessary to implement a comprehensive and effective regulation system is enormous, as the government has to establish the precise output solutions for all pollution activities, so regulation can only be partially successful.

The first significant regulatory act was the 1956 Clean Air Act. This was intended to address the issue of smog, which had constituted an important health hazard in the post-war years. Smog was caused by the burning of coal, the particulate matter resulting from the combustion becoming suspended in the atmosphere when there was fog. The Clean Air Act proved to be most effective in substantially reducing the incidence of smog and was followed by a further act in 1968. However, this coincided with the gradual transition from home fires to central heating and the phasing out of steam locomotives, plus the increasing use by industry of electricity from the Central Electricity Generating Board, rather than providing power from stationary steam engines in factories. The net result was that technological change was facilitating reduced emissions of the carbon particulates responsible for the smog.

Britain was the first nation in the world to produce electricity from nuclear power, and from the 1950s embarked on a programme of constructing first-generation magnesium oxide (Magnox) reactors, of which eleven were built. There was great optimism in those days that nuclear power would prove to be a safe and very cheap form of energy. The technology was developed further in this country and by the 1970s Britain was introducing seven new advanced gas-cooled reactors (AGRs). These were supposed to have various technical advantages over the water-cooled reactors developed in the USA, including the ability to be refuelled while they were producing electricity. Over-optimism meant that in practice they were not as efficient as claimed, and the government decided to start building the American Westinghouse-designed pressurised water reactors (PWRs) to add to the existing stock of Magnox and

AGRs. However, in 1979 at Three Mile Island in the USA, just such a PWR reactor suffered a catastrophic failure, and this was followed seven years later by another catastrophic reactor failure, this time in the USSR at Chernobyl, and Britain's programme of construction was halted. The existing reactors were maintained, but with the privatisation of the energy industry in the 1980s (see Chapter 11), nuclear electricity production was kept in a separate company, now called British Energy, by which time a fifth of total electricity production was nuclear. By the end of the century the Magnox reactors were near the end of their lives and decommissioning began. This is a dangerous and expensive process as they remain highly radioactive; it also means that a declining proportion of electricity is being generated by nuclear energy. Only four of these remained in 2006, and are all to be decommissioned by 2010. The New Labour government of Tony Blair has toyed with the idea of constructing new nuclear reactors to replace the Magnox stations.

By the 1980s environmental groups such as Friends of the Earth and Greenpeace were promoting environmental concerns strongly, and the Secretary of State for the Environment in Margaret Thatcher's Conservative government, Nicholas Ridley, commissioned the economist David Pearce to develop a policy to address these concerns. He advocated that the government should intervene in the market and place a Pigouvian tax (named after the economist A. C. Pigou) upon the polluter equal to the marginal external cost. This would mean that the firm's supply curve would become the marginal social cost curve, and the externality would be internalised; that is, the pollution would be accounted for in the cost structure of the firm (see Figure 13.1).

The marginal external cost (the cost of the environmental damage) is borne by both the producer and the consumer of the product which is causing the pollution. How this cost is divided between the producer and the consumer is determined by the own price elasticity of demand for the product. The more elastic the demand, the greater the proportion of the cost burdened by the producer (see Figure 13.2). The greater the degree of competition in the industrial sector, the more elastic demand for each firm's product will be; so government competition policy can help to ensure that the consumer is protected from paying for the costs of pollution. This also means that as industry now shoulders the burden for a high proportion of the environmental tax, it has a pecuniary incentive to look for technical solutions to reduce environmentally damaging emissions, and so reduce the tax burden which it endures.

Figure 13.1

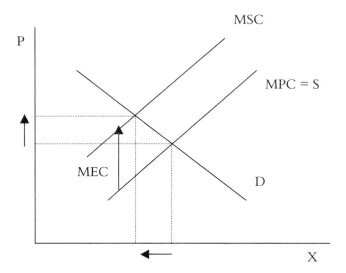

Price (P) is on the Y-axis, with the quantity of some good or service X on the X-axis. The firm's marginal private cost (MPC) is its supply curve S. The marginal social cost (MSC) curve lies above the MPC as it includes the entire cost of the good to society including the cost of the pollution, viz the marginal external cost (MEC). Thus MPC + MEC = MSC. If government sets a tax equal to the MEC so that the firm's supply curve is raised to become the MSC curve, then the price and output solution change to where the MSC curve intercepts the demand curve (D), whereas without the tax this solution is where the MPC curve intercepts D. By levying the tax the market price is raised and the increased cost lowers output, which also helps to reduce pollution. Thus the externality is internalised – the market for the good pays for the environmental damage.

There are, however, some problems with government setting a tax equal to the marginal external cost of a production externality, the most significant being the problem of non-marketable goods. In the example of the chemical plant, we assumed that the river was fished commercially, and thus the environmental cost of the pollution could be measured by the value of the lost income to the fishermen, that is, the market value of the reduced fish catch, and so the government could set a tax equal to that amount. However, pollution often damages the environment in a way which is difficult to measure in financial terms. Suppose that the chemical plant is in a very picturesque area, and that the discharged effluent reduces the amount of wildlife and damages the appearance of the river and its immediate surrounding area. The wildlife and the picturesque beauty of the environment are non-marketable goods; in other words, there is no market value which can be used to determine the magnitude of the tax which government needs to set

Figure 13.2

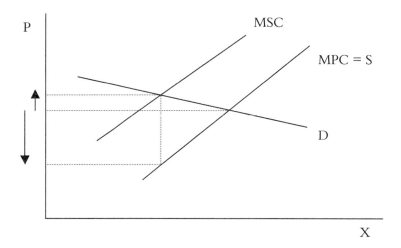

With a demand curve which is more elastic, more of the pollution tax is borne by the producer. The length of both arrows taken together on the price axis (P) represents the total MEC and thus, *ex hypothesi*, the tax. But the proportion of the tax borne by the consumer is represented by the top arrow (the amount by which the market price of the good has risen). The proportion of the tax borne by the producer is the lower arrow (the amount by which the firm's revenue has fallen).

in order to internalise the externality. The method which Pearce advocated to deal with this problem was to carry out a survey and simply ask the public how much they believed that these natural features of the environment were worth, and set the tax accordingly. Another problem of imposing a tax equal to the marginal external cost of economic activity is to do with the fact that the government has to develop a bureaucracy to accumulate the necessary information, monitor the activities of firms and levy the tax. This itself imposes an additional cost burden upon society. The net result of these problems was that the government shelved the proposal.

An alternative solution is to employ the notion of property rights to address the pollution problem, as advocated by the American theorists Ronald Coase and E. J. Mishan. This would function in the following manner: with every acquisition of property would come legally enforceable rights to good air quality, water quality, etc. The problem with this is that any violation of these rights must be pursued through the law courts, but it is the wealthy (including wealthy polluting businesses) who are in a stronger position than the poor to win court cases. The government could take over the provision of all activities which cause pollution; but this would amount to nationalisation and public ownership of most economic activities with the consequent misallocation of resources, in short, economic inefficiency.

However, Britain continued with its policy of environmental control through regulation. In 1987 Her Majesty's Inspectorate of Pollution was formed by merging the inspectorates for air pollution, water pollution, pollution by radioactive materials and chemicals, and pollution by hazardous waste. Two years later the National Rivers Authority was created, which is responsible for pollution control, flood defences and fishing controls, and also has responsibility for managing the recreational uses of the rivers. The 1990 Environmental Protection Act introduced local authority responsibility to recycle domestic waste.

The Advisory Committee on Hazardous Substances, composed of scientists, became responsible for analysing the risks associated with the use of hazardous substances. This body was to make recommendations on reducing such risks while being aware of the affect on business competitiveness. No industrial society can function with zero emissions of hazardous substances; the purpose of this regulatory body was to balance risk against the level of economic growth. The body was given statutory powers to set limits in terms of parts per million of hazardous substances permissible in the environment, with non-compliant businesses liable to prosecution. Increasingly Britain has been obliged to adopt European Union regulations on such environmental matters.

In May 1996 the Conservative government introduced a bio-diversity targets initiative, which involved the improvement of all sites of special scientific interest (SSSIs). These are sites, with statutory protection, where certain flora and fauna of special interest which require conservation are prevalent. Those government departments which own SSSIs were required under the initiative to develop pertinent plans for site improvements, and bio-diversity plans were also required for the refurbishment of government buildings.

When it came to power in May 1997, Tony Blair's Labour government merged the Department of the Environment with the Department of Transport to create the Department of the Environment, Transport and the Regions (DETR), as these had all been deemed low priority issues (see Chapter 10). The deputy Prime Minister, John Prescott, was put in charge. But further reorganisation resulted in a demerger of this department, and environmental issues were then merged with what had been another low priority issue, agriculture. This resulted in the creation of the Department for Environment, Food and Rural Affairs (DEFRA). Blair then raised the priority of environmental issues and put a capable politician, Margaret Beckett, in charge.

This Department introduced the UK Chemical Stakeholder Forum to address environmental issues. This is made up of scientists, industrialists, trade unionists, environmentalists, environmental protection groups and conser-vationists. The official purpose of this forum is to bring all of the pertinent interest groups together to create a balanced judgement: in reality the industrialists will want higher limits on emissions for commercial reasons than the environmental groups would wish for, and so the function of the forum is to establish some compromise set of limits.

The Blair government is signatory to the Kyoto protocol, an international agreement to reduce the six principal types of greenhouse gas emissions which adversely affect the environment and cause global warming. The protocol was introduced in December 1997, and was ratified by 150 countries in all. It stipulates specific targets and timetables for greenhouse gas emission reductions by the signatory countries up until 2012. Britain has committed to an ambitious target of reducing such emissions by 20 per cent below the 1990 level by 2010, though it is unlikely to achieve this. However, the USA has notably failed to ratify the protocol, saying it is committed to technical solutions to emission problems not constraints on industrial output.

An environmental tax called the climate change levy was introduced by the Blair government in April 2001. This tax is imposed on the energy consumption of both private sector businesses and the public sector, and is intended to encourage energy efficiency. It is revenue neutral, so it is accompanied by a reduction in the national insurance contributions which employers are obliged to make (see Chapter 6). Twelve months later DEFRA introduced the UK Emissions Trading Scheme (ETS). This scheme was designed to target greenhouse gases. It is based on a scheme which President Bill Clinton introduced in the USA, and is the principal element of the UK Climate Change Programme, which is intended to reduce greenhouse gas emissions. The scheme enables businesses responsible for greenhouse gas emissions to purchase and to trade emissions allowances. At the same time, participants commit themselves to reducing their emissions in accordance with government targets in return for government finance. Under the scheme the emission reduction targets became more stringent by annual increments between 2002 and 2006.

A substantial number of organisations have participated in the British scheme and emissions have been reduced under it, but there is evidence that the organisations which have reduced their emissions the most are those with the lowest abatement costs, and that the initial emissions reductions were achieved because targets became more stringent in the later stages of the scheme. It is also clear that some emissions reductions would have happened anyway without the scheme. However, the experience British organisations gained in managing greenhouse gas emissions through the scheme's reporting and verification systems has had a beneficial effect. But the British scheme had a limited life span, whereas the American scheme is open ended; this is partly because the British scheme was intended to act as a pilot for the European Union ETS, which was introduced in 2005.

The Blair government's energy White Paper commits Britain to reduce its carbon dioxide emissions by 60 per cent by 2050. Given this long time scale, yet the short time horizon of any government, the target means little; it is impossible to predict economic growth and technological change over such a period, or to influence future governments, thus this is no more than propaganda. There has been some introduction of renewable energy production: an isolated number of wind turbines generating electricity, and experimentation in wave power. Neither of these will generate more than a small fraction of Britain's electricity in the foreseeable future: only 500 megawatts of electricity were being generated in 2005 from a couple of farms of wind turbines and a few isolated examples scattered across the country, though eighteen more farms are proposed. Yet the construction of these, the one active and viable option, has been opposed on environmental grounds!

Overseas development

In order to undertake development and promote environmental issues on an international scale, the government created the Department for International Development, responsible for providing grant aid to developing countries. This grant aid is directed at less developed countries (LDCs), and the very poorest countries in the world, the least developed countries. Until recently the head of this department was only a minister of state (that is, not of Cabinet rank). Tony Blair elevated the status of the departmental head to secretary of state. This marked Blair's promotion of this policy to further his attempts to make a place in history for himself by solving Africa's economic problems.

Since 1945 Britain's aid budget has exceeded those of the major industrial countries, with the exceptions of the USA, Japan and (West) Germany. During the Thatcher period of government Britain's aid budget declined overall (at constant prices), though it has increased again under Blair. Unsurprisingly, given Britain's status as a former colonial power, its aid budget has been spent predominantly on its former colonial possessions.

Bilateral aid, which takes the form of a relationship between a donor country and a recipient country, has accounted for over three-fifths of the total British aid budget. The donor country's economy benefits from bilateral aid because of the high degree to which aid projects are 'tied' to the donor country's industry. This means that the recipient country must purchase what it needs for the aid project from the donor country; thus (in a bilateral agreement with Britain) if tied aid is used to finance some infrastructure project in a developing country, a high proportion of that aid will be received by British contractors. To secure value for money for British taxpayers, a system of competitive tendering was usually used, organised by the Crown Agents.

From 1945 until 1979 the policy of tying aid in Britain was to some extent linked to the creation of demand for the output of those British industries where there was under-utilised capacity; or for industries in structural decline. This changed with the Thatcher government, which no longer supported such industries.

Mixed financing, where aid is augmented by commercial loans, which may be guaranteed by the British government, has been another element of British overseas development policy in the last few decades. This is viable only for the more advanced developing countries, as only they are capable of attracting commercial loans. However, Britain has insisted on a relatively small aid element relative to the credit component by comparison with that required by most donor countries.

Britain has also linked aid provision to trading agreements, in a system known as the aid and trade provision (ATP). The ATP has tended to benefit the most developed of the LDCs, as they have a more advanced trading structure and have benefited particularly in respect of manufacturing, energy and communications. ATP projects have resulted in substantial orders for British businesses, with large companies benefiting the most, though some small sub-contractors have also gained business, and subsequent orders have been placed as a direct consequence. However, quite a few of these contracts would have occurred without the British government's involvement under the ATP, and such contracts have constituted only a very small proportion of British industrial output. Another problem of the ATP, as a House of Commons select committee pointed out, is that the commercial aspects of the trading relationship dominate over the development aid aspect, and so aid has been misallocated in some cases simply to enhance trade.

Multilateral aid, which is provided by donor countries to international agencies before being dispersed to recipient countries, has accounted for less than two-fifths of the total British aid budget. Over a third of Britain's multilateral aid budget has been spent via the World Bank and over 40 per cent via the EU. It is a general rule that contracts for development projects financed by multilateral agencies are put out to international competitive tender, but only those firms which are located in the member countries of these multilateral agencies can tender. Thus, unlike bilateral aid, there can be no tying; contracts are awarded on the basis of the international com-petitiveness of the tendering businesses. Yet, counter-intuitively, contracts have not necessarily gone predominantly to companies in the most productive countries, with British and Italian companies enjoying a particularly high proportion of such contracts. The reason Britain benefits from such multilateral-aid-financed orders is because of its Commonwealth links with many developing countries which were formerly its imperial possessions.

In recent years, consultancy contracts have increasingly become significant in aid provision, as they lead to demand for manufactured goods. Thus donor countries have deemed it important to gain such consultancy contracts as their own manufacturers then enjoy a higher probability of securing orders.

Given the relatively small proportion of total development funds which are provided to the developing world by grant aid, it is commercial loans which provide the bulk of the development finance. This is also received by newly industrialising countries (NICs), which are more advanced than the LDCs, as well as by the LDCs themselves. NICs have a manufacturing base, whereas LDCs tend to be reliant on agriculture and the extractive industries, which provide less income than manufacturing.

In the late 1970s, the G7 countries (the seven largest economies in the world) used a mix of expansionary fiscal policy and contractionary monetary policy to address stagflation (see Chapter 5). This resulted in a substantial rise in the interest rate and so, unintentionally, the debt repayments of developing countries rose substantially as well. In mid-1982 Mexico was obliged to default on its foreign debt repayments as a result, and it was followed by some twenty-two other developing countries. Since then real emphasis has been placed upon the significance of addressing the international debt problems.

Given the massive indebtedness of developing countries to commercial banks in the advanced industrial countries, the latter had a vested interest in rescheduling the debts in order that repayments should resume and thus prevent a major banking collapse in the developed world. To that end, in 1989 Nicholas Brady, US Secretary of the Treasury, introduced such a plan and so made it easier for developing countries to repay their debt by extending the period of repayment. Since then many developing countries have been required to concentrate upon generating trade surpluses in order to pay off debt and to reduce domestic economic development as a result. Thus there has been a net transfer of resources from developing countries to advanced industrial ones; in consequence LDCs' real per capita incomes have risen on average by less than 2 per cent per annum since 1982, which is half the growth rate of the previous fifteen years, and in some cases they actually fell. Across these countries, aggregate incomes would have been approximately $2 trillion greater had it not been for the consequences of the debt crisis; this is about $3,500 per head.

Everyone accepts that in order to restore LDCs' growth and credit-worthiness, the negative net resource transfers require reversing. However, there are differences of view between economists regarding whether economic development in the LDCs can be stimulated without first reducing the degree of their indebtedness. Some economists argue that debt reduction is necessary in order to enable more of LDC government budgets to be devoted to development rather than debt repayment. Other economists argue that substantially increasing investment in LDCs through additional aid would increase real per capita incomes despite the debt repayments, and thus aid should not be primarily directed at debt relief. However, the magnitude of the total cumulative debt of developing countries is so vast that to write it off would require between $35 billion and $55 billion annually.

All heads of government wish to define their place in history, and for Tony Blair it was to be through his programme to end poverty in Africa and deal with global environmental problems. His quid pro quo for supporting George Bush's policy of regime change in Iraq was to induce the Bush presidency to support this grand policy, because it could not happen without American involvement. But the policy was only given limited support by the Bush administration, which had no real interest in either issue.

During 2005 Blair employed his presidency of the G8 countries (the G7's successor organisation, which now includes Russia) to encourage them to address the poverty situation in Africa. His plan was for these countries to finance an economic package to address the fundamental issues of economic growth, poverty, eliminating unfair trading barriers and increasing monetary resources in developing countries. To this end the G8, meeting at Gleneagles, announced an increase of their aid commitment by $50 billion; however, they failed to set a deadline for implementation. The agreement should double total aid to approximately $100 billion a year by 2010, of which 50 per cent will be received by Africa. But, without structural reform of the institutions of governance of the developing countries, this money may be misallocated.

The G8 at Gleneagles also agreed to implement the Heavily Indebted Poor Countries (HIPC) programme. They committed themselves to spending $70 billion on debt relief for twenty-seven countries in all, of which all but four are African. This is intended to reduce their indebtedness by an average of approximately two-thirds. The programme was to be extended to permit another ten eligible HIPC countries to receive in excess of $30 billion. However, the commitment to all of these figures is no more than a statement of intent, and there is already evidence that donor countries will prove unable or unwilling to meet these obligations.

On environmental issues, agreement by the G8 was limited because the USA is opposed to cutting its economic growth rates in order to reduce pollution. However, the USA did accept, along with the other G8 countries, that global warming was a product of industrial activity, a measure sufficient to prevent France from issuing another communiqué without the USA. But the USA ensured that the communiqué said no more than that we should 'act with resolve and urgency', committing to no action. There was also an agreement in principle to ending the developed countries' export subsidies in agriculture, but no agreement on timing.

Conclusion

It has been Tony Blair's grand plan to establish his personal place in the pantheon of great international statesmen which, more than any other consideration, has elevated these policies on the international stage. But in order for such policies to have significant effect, the USA and the EU have to endorse and finance them. There has been some recalcitrant behaviour in the EU, and the USA is little interested in either issue.

14

Britain and its relationship with European unification

Introduction

The relationship with the process of European unification has been the most difficult long-term policy issue for Britain, and yet the most vital. The fundamental impediment is that Britain lacks the wherewithal to act independently from other major nations, and must choose between supporting either the EU or the USA, a decision, however, which it refuses to make.

After the Second World War, European political philosophers such as Jean Monnet, who would become the architect of the European Union, and Robert Schuman, the French Foreign Minister, reflected on the causes of warfare. They concluded that the principal cause was the notion of nationalism, and so the solution to war was to subsume nation states within a supra-national institution. The first institutional manifestation of this notion was the European Coal and Steel Community (ECSC), created in 1951, whose members were France, West Germany, Italy and the Benelux countries (Belgium, the Netherlands and Luxembourg). The purpose of this organisation was to bring the production and distribution of the principal materials required for prosecuting a war under a supra-national organisation, and so deny any one country the facility of independent access to these materials, and thus the ability to prosecute a war.

A more encompassing organisation integrating the economies of these nation states would create economic and political interdependence and thus subsume nationalism in a more profound way. The Messina proposal for a European Economic Community (EEC) resulted in the Treaty of Rome in 1957, with the ECSC members becoming its originators. The EEC was later renamed the European Community (EC) and subsequently the European Union (EU).

At the end of the Second World War Britain still had a global Empire, it had strategic forces which it could project worldwide, and its dire economic state was perceived to be transitory. British foreign and economic policy interests were predominantly oriented towards its colonies and the Commonwealth, which were in Africa, Central and South America, the Pacific, the Near and Far East, plus Canada. However, Britain was reliant upon the USA for its defence. Britain thus saw itself as a 'superpower' with little interest in Europe, and no interest in subsuming itself within a European supra-national institution.

Winston Churchill supported European unification to prevent a Third World War but insisted Britain should not be part of it. He posited three spheres of interest: Britain and the Commonwealth, the USA and (continental) Europe, intersecting like a Venn diagram: each with overlapping interests, but nevertheless separate. This line of thinking was shared by the post-war Labour government of Clement Attlee, which declined to join the ECSC when invited so to do. The Conservative Prime Minister Anthony Eden would later decline to participate in the EEC for the same reasons.

However, Britain was subject to an 'illusion of grandeur'. This was all to change with the Suez crisis (see Chapter 12), when the USA intervened to stop British policy, in consequence of which the illusion disappeared. Superpowers can act on the international stage largely as they please; as Britain had been prevented from so doing it became very clear that it was not such a power. With this recognition, an impediment to British membership of the EEC had also gone. A few years later, by 1960, when the cost of policing and administering the Empire was exceeding the economic benefits of maintaining it, and the legitimate aspiration for independence among Britain's colonies was growing strongly, the Macmillan government initiated a policy of dismantling the Empire (see Chapter 12), thus removing another impediment to British membership of the EEC.

It became clear that the British economy was never going to be restored to its pre-eminence of the late nineteenth century, and with the fastest economic growth being in advanced industrial countries which traded with similar countries (the Commonwealth was predominantly Third World), the case for accelerating economic growth through membership of the EEC, with the West German 'economic miracle' driving growth, became overwhelming.

However, having refused to join the EEC ab initio, in 1960 Britain set up the European Free Trade Area with Austria, Denmark, Norway, Portugal, Sweden and Switzerland. It was a purely free trade organisation, and too small to offer the stimulus to economic growth that Britain really required. In consequence Britain formally applied for EEC membership in 1962, but it was only interested in free trade, not political unity. In 1963 France (principally the President, Charles de Gaulle) prevented Britain from joining because it feared that Britain would be a conduit for American influence and was not committed to the European ideal of political unity.

The Labour government of Harold Wilson tried again to join the EEC with Foreign Secretary George Brown leading the negotiations, but Britain was again rebuffed in 1967 for the same set of reasons. By the 1970s French opposition to British membership of the European Community had ended, principally because de Gaulle had resigned as President in 1969, dying the following year. The British Prime Minister, Edward Heath, sounded out his replacement, Georges Pompidou, and negotiations began for British membership. Heath signed the agreement for British entry into the EC in 1972, which became active from 1 January 1973.

The Labour government, elected in 1974, gave the British people a referendum on EEC membership the following year, ostensibly because this was a momentous constitutional change, and the former government had not asked the British electorate. In reality it was because the Labour Party was split over the question of EEC membership, and putting the question to the electorate was a way of deciding the matter. In the referendum the British electorate voted in favour of continuing membership of the EEC by a clear majority.

Although the basic impediments to British membership of the EEC had gone, there was considerable political opposition to membership based on the notion of national sovereignty. The more political integration there was in the EEC, the less control Britain would have over its national destiny. In 1979 the members of the European Parliament (see Addendum) became directly elected by the electorate of each of the EEC member states. This took some power from the Westminster Parliament as it gave the European Parliament democratic legitimacy. This created an ambiguity for the anti-EEC politicians: one of the reasons for opposing European unification was because of the democratic deficit, the lack of electoral accountability of EEC institutions, but make the parliament directly elected and you vitiate this argument.

Within the EU, each nation contributes to the budget in proportion to the size of its economy, with over half of the entire budget being spent on the Common Agricultural Policy (CAP). When the EEC was created in 1957 the original member states had substantial agricultural sectors. These mainly comprised small family-owned farms with a mix of dairy and arable production. These farms lacked the economies of scale of the vast American farms of the Midwest, and would not survive in a commercial market. The agricultural lobby was a significant political one as it was numerically very large. It was fear of unemployment, demographic change and the physical changes to the countryside of introducing highly efficient commercial farming which drove the development of the CAP.

Under the CAP, the European Commission (see Addendum) agreed to purchase all excess food stocks in order to guarantee farm incomes, and protectionist import duties prevented competition from agricultural industries outside the EEC. The Commission was then to release these stocks onto the market when there was a poor harvest. But guaranteeing farm incomes simply encouraged over-production, so in December 1993 the EU, as it had been renamed by then, agreed to reduce the CAP's guaranteed prices for agricultural produce by 30 per cent. Also it was decided to develop supplementary income payments to be determined by farm size and output. These payments were contingent upon farmers participating in the 'set-aside' scheme, where all but the smallest farmers were obliged not to use, or to set aside, 15 per cent of their acreage with the provision of grants for compensation. This was a measure intended to reduce agricultural output. The set-aside land was to be employed for forestry or for some recreational use and was linked directly with environmental considerations. The purpose of these arrangements was to move agricultural prices closer to internationally competitive levels and therefore to help consumers and reduce export subsidies, but they increased the burden on taxpayers.

These measures were further reformed in 1999, the principal motivating factor being the increased cost of the enlargement of the EU. These reforms were a continuation of the 1993 reforms with further shifts from price support to direct payments. It also reduced EU financing of the CAP from 100 per cent to 75 per cent, with the remainder financed by national governments. Furthermore, EU farmers are now subsidised to act as caretakers of the natural environment and not just to produce food.

As Britain had a relatively small and efficient agricultural sector, when it entered the EEC it became the second largest net contributor to the budget, while it was only the third largest economy. In 1984, when Margaret Thatcher was Prime Minister, she negotiated a budget rebate to reduce Britain's total budgetary commitment. This was not achieved through reform of the CAP, but through an ex gratia lump sum annual repayment. The rebate equates to 66 per cent of the net contributions of Britain in the previous year. As the EU budget rises, so does the rebate, and in 2005 it stood at approximately €4.5 billion per annum. Britain is now the largest net contributor to the EU before the rebate is now taken into account (Germany is next) and constitutes the second largest economy in the EU, having overtaken France. In December 2005, under the British presidency of the EU, Tony Blair reduced the size of the British budget rebate by £1 billion a year in negotiations with the EU countries. This was generally seen as a defeat for him, as he surrendered part of the rebate to the new entrants into the EU but did not secure anything in return more than a commitment to review the CAP. However, France was adamant in its opposition to further CAP reform.

The EU also has a Common Fisheries Policy (CFP), which originated in the Treaty of Rome in 1957 but was not introduced until 1983. Although each member state of the EU has an exclusive twelve-mile zone which only its own vessels may fish, fishing vessels from all member states have access to a zone outside the twelve-mile limit which extends to 200 nautical miles from the EU coastline. A quota system of total allowable catches, with quotas specified for each country, is employed in an attempt to sustain fish stocks. The CFP also operates a price control and a grant provision system. Just as with the CAP, this encouraged over-production and the CFP was reformed in 1992 and again in 2002 to protect fish stocks. The latter reforms resulted in the scrapping of grants for fishing vessel construction and premiums were raised for the decommissioning of old vessels. Also plans were introduced to protect specific endangered species.

Thatcher was a nationalist and opposed in principle to the loss of sovereignty which Britain would suffer by further political integration with Europe. However, in 1986 she signed the Single European Act, which, inter alia, evolved qualified majority voting (QMV) for use by the Council of Ministers (now the Council of the European Union – see Addendum), covering many policy issues in the EC (though for major measures unanimity is still required). This meant that no nation could veto these particular issues, and so weakened British national sovereignty. We take up QMV in detail in the Addendum.

Thatcher had signed the Single European Act because she recognised that in EC negotiations it was necessary to support measures which other governments wanted in return for their support for the measures she wanted. Part of the Act concerned the single market, which became active at the beginning of 1993. This gave free movement to all goods, services, capital and labour in the EU. This was consistent with Thatcher's free-market principles and she was strongly in favour.

John Major replaced Thatcher as Conservative Prime Minister with the expectation that he would unite the party, which was deeply divided over the European issue. However, he had no views of his own and lacked the ability to achieve unity. He negotiated the 'opt-out' of the Social Chapter of the Maastricht treaty of 1992, which committed member states to social legislation including the introduction of a national minimum wage (see Chapter 11). The Conservatives split themselves over the Maastricht treaty, and this would play a role in their general election defeat in 1997, as did the ejection of sterling from the European Monetary System in 1992 (see Chapter 5).

When Blair replaced Major he negotiated an 'opt-in' to the Social Chapter, and thus a national minimum wage was introduced in Britain (see Chapter 11). Blair also wanted Britain to adopt the single currency, as he saw this as a bargaining counter to encourage the rest of the EU to accept British policies concerning flexible labour markets, reforms to the CAP and widening (more member states) rather than deepening (more political integration) of the EU. Blair promised a referendum for the British people on euro membership. However, opinion polls showed (and continue to show) that the British would not vote in favour, and Blair does not believe that he can alter this stance, therefore there has been no referendum. An additional problem for Blair is opposition from within his own government on this matter (see Chapter 5).

Blair's more constructive approach to the EU has resulted in British participation in some cooperative areas of EU defence and foreign policy. The Balkan wars of the 1990s showed how weak European governments were when they tried to act alone. That experience encouraged governments to forge a common EU foreign policy, so that they would act together more effectively in future crises. In 1999 EU governments, with the support of the Blair government, agreed to set up an EU defence policy to support their common foreign policy. The first significant effect of this was when in 2003 the EU undertook peacekeeping missions in the Democratic Republic of the Congo and Macedonia, and then in 2004 it took over more demanding peacekeeping responsibilities in Bosnia from NATO.

In April 2004 European defence ministers agreed that, by 2007, the EU should have available for deployment within two weeks' notice nine 'battle groups', each consisting of 1,500 troops. The ministers have additionally agreed to a capabilities '2010 headline goal', a plan which commits them to acquire a variety of very advanced materiel, including guided missiles, unmanned aircraft and transport planes, by 2010. To help them cooperate in purchasing and developing military equipment, the EU governments agreed to set up a European defence agency, which started functioning in 2004. This agency lobbies EU member states to increase expenditure on new military materiel and to build a more open and competitive European market for defence goods.

In order to establish closer political integration in the EU, a written constitution was drawn up with the agreement of the governments of the member states. Ratification of the constitution was required by all member states before it was introduced. Some states chose to perform this function by taking a vote in their national legislatures, but France and the Netherlands both held national referenda in 2005. Both referenda resulted in a 'no' vote and so the constitution was rendered defunct, enabling the Blair government to avoid holding the referendum in Britain which he had promised, a vote which he would very probably have lost. These 'no' votes have currently halted the integration process, and Blair attempted to take the initiative left in the power vacuum to press for the British-sponsored reforms mentioned above.

France, Germany and the European Union

France and Germany are the most significant of the EU countries as together they were principally responsible for developing European unification in the beginning, and driving the process of integration subsequently. Thus a consideration of French and German motives brings the British position into sharper relief.

France wanted to exercise hegemonic influence, but the post-war order constrained it as it lacked a sufficiently large economy to function independently as a superpower, and because of the overriding hegemonic influence of the USA. West Germany had a larger economy but was subject to an American-imposed foreign and defence policy. France wanted to tie West Germany politically to the centre of Europe in order to prevent it from precipitating another conflict in the continent. Charles de Gaulle sought a rapprochement with West Germany after the Second World War in order to establish a Franco-German axis which would drive the process of European unification and create a third superpower between what de Gaulle called the 'unbridled capitalism' of the USA and the communism of the USSR. In the 1980s François Mitterrand, the then French President, proposed the notion of three concentric circles to illustrate his vision of Europe: France and West Germany in the innermost circle, the rest of the EU in the second circle, and the rest of Europe in the outer circle. Thus France and Germany would continue to be central to European unification.

West Germany wanted to be protected from itself, to ensure that no military dictatorship took power there again, and consequently Germans saw European unification as a guarantee of this. Also, West Germany wanted to exercise a degree of political power commensurate with its economic size, something which it had been unable to do because the nation had been divided, under American hegemony in the west and Soviet hegemony in the east. Thus Mitterrand, and Helmut Kohl, the German Chancellor in the 1980s and 1990s, decided to start a programme of unifying France and West Germany at the centre of Europe, so establishing their own places in political history.

Since the collapse of the USSR, the partial withdrawal of the USA from Europe and the consequent reunification of Germany, it is now possible that Germany may increasingly extend its own hegemonic powers eastwards. It has wanted to do this since at least the 1890s. It failed to achieve this by military means in two world wars, but can now do so peacefully through its economic influence. Germany has been increasingly undertaking foreign direct investment and providing financial loans to eastern Europe. This, and the importance of German markets for demanding goods from eastern European businesses, creates an economic dependence of eastern Europe on Germany. Economic dependence causes political dependence. As most of today's Germans were born after the Second World War, they feel less fear concerning their own past. This has created a tension in German policy: it is still officially committed to European unification (to the relief of the French) but in the long run, Germany may wish to dominate Europe economically and politically without France.

Conclusion

Britain is no nearer now to making a fundamental decision between allegiance either to the EU or to the USA than it was in 1945. Allegiance to the USA is a very one-sided relationship. Allegiance to the EU would give Britain some leverage in international affairs although this is necessarily constrained by the other EU members, particularly France and Germany. This failure to ally itself with the EU will continue to ensure that Britain's international influence remains extremely limited. Britain has attempted to play an honest-broker role between the USA and the EU, but neither is interested and they will liaise directly without Britain's mediation.

Addendum

The institutions of the
European Union

The principal institutions of the European Union are the Commission, the Parliament, the Council of the European Union (also known as the Council of Ministers) and the Court of Justice. If we were to consider these institutions as analogous to those of Britain's national government, then the Commission would be the civil service, the Parliament is of course the legislature, the Council would be the Cabinet and the Court a supreme constitutional court. However, it is not quite as simple as that. The founders of the European ideal and the architect of these institutions, Jean Monnet, conceived of the Commission as a centre for government, and so it is highly politicised and has a degree of executive authority greater than that of a national civil service.

The European Commission

This is the largest and most significant of the EU's institutions. It is located in Brussels and comprises the President of the Commission and the heads of the Commission's departments, the commissioners. The President is selected by the governments of the member states from nominees proposed by some of those member states. The commissioners are selected by national governments and are usually politicians with experience in their national political systems. Before enlargement, two commissioners were provided from each of the larger EU member states (France, Germany, Italy, Spain and the UK) and one each from the smaller ones. Since the membership of the EU was extended to twenty-five states in May 2004, each state contributes just one commissioner. The national governments must then collectively decide which commissioner is allocated to which department.

Commissioners are expected to maintain efficient channels of communication with their national governments and with other pertinent bodies in order to ensure that the Commission does not propose policies which national governments would not approve. However, they are also obliged to take an oath of allegiance to the EU and to refrain from accepting any political directives from their respective national governments or indeed any outside body. This creates an ambiguous relationship between commissioners and the national governments which nominated them, for it is hard for them not to be influenced by their government's policies.

Each commissioner is responsible for running a department, for example transport or agriculture, and each has a chief of staff and a supporting personal staff. It is this body of people which is collectively responsible for developing policies. Each department has a large civil service comprised of a wide range of administrative personnel, such as interpreters, research scientists and sundry clerical staff. The head of this administration is known as the director-general. If we compare this structure to that of the British national government, then the commissioner is equivalent to a secretary of state, but is more independent and more difficult to dismiss, and the director-general is equivalent to a permanent under-secretary of state, a department's most senior civil servant.

The size of the departments or directorates-general varies considerably depending upon their particular function; by far the largest is agriculture, which in the past has been responsible for spending over 50 per cent of the total EU budget. Others such as transport and regional policy are quite small. The Commission has no tax-raising powers of its own but receives all its income from the governments of the member states proportionate to their size. This enables those states to exercise control over the Commission.

The principal functions of the Commission are to develop policy ab initio, to implement these policies (together with the member states) if they are assented to by the Council, and to undertake expenditure functions via the Regional Fund, the Social Fund, and the Common Agricultural Policy. The Commission is also responsible for the Customs Union, the system of tariffs and quotas which are imposed on goods and services imported from outside the EU. These trade restrictions are quite substantial and are intended to protect indigenous EU industry. There are some concessions made to trade with some former colonial possessions of member states in Africa and elsewhere.

The Commission is very open to lobbying; many organisations either actively lobby in Brussels or, in the case of the larger ones, have permanent facilities there. They include businesses and public and non-profit organisations. Many of those which operate across a number of EU countries have realised that lobbying the Commission is more effective than lobbying national governments. Also, given the more socialist orientation to policy in Brussels than in Westminster, British trade unions have taken to lobbying the Commission rather more than the British government.

The Commission is obliged to ensure that all member states comply with the rules laid down in the EU treaties. If a member state, a local authority or a commercial company based in a member state violates the provisions of these treaties, then it is incumbent upon the Commission to instruct it to desist. This is usually sufficient, but on the occasions where it is not, the Commission asks the European Court of Justice to take up the issue (see below).

When Britain joined the EEC, the Cabinet Office had already set up the European Secretariat to assist the government in liaising with the Commission. British government departments also liaise directly with the Commission.

The Council of the European Union

Formerly known as the Council of Ministers, this is the executive body of the EU; only with its say are policy proposals put into effect. However, further political integration in the EU has resulted in the development of 'co-decision' between the Council and the Parliament. We explore this when we discuss the Parliament and again when we look at the decision-making process below.

The Council comprises a Cabinet minister from each member state, responsible nationally for the policy issue currently under discussion. Thus, if agricultural policy is being discussed by the Council, then the Council will be composed of the agriculture ministers from the governments of each member state, if it is financial policy, then the Council consists of the member states' finance ministers, and so on. In some cases national governments may send more than one minister, and ministers are usually accompanied by senior civil servants. The range of different policy issues discussed by the Council is as follows: General Affairs and External Relations; Economic and Financial Affairs; Justice and Home Affairs; Employment, Social Policy, Health and Consumer Affairs; Competitiveness; Transport, Telecommunications and Energy; Agriculture and Fisheries; Environment; Education, Youth and Culture.

The presidency of the Council (not to be confused with the President of the Commission) is held by the head of government or state of each member on a six-monthly rotational basis. The order is determined alphabetically, approximately by the international identification plates of road vehicles, except that Britain is identified as UK rather than GB, and Denmark (DK) precedes Germany (D).

When the Council meets to discuss major policy issues, which it does a maximum of four times a year, it comprises the heads of government or state and the President of the Commission and is referred to as the European Council. It is convened by the current President of the Council, who develops a policy agenda in cooperation with the Commission and the governments of the other member states.

The reason for the Council's structure, and for its executive role, is that the member states wish to control the EU, not have the EU control them.

The European Parliament

The European Parliament or Assembly is located in Strasbourg. It is composed of members of the European Parliament (MEPs), directly elected since 1979 by universal franchise from each member state; prior to that date the Parliament was not directly elected but consisted of delegates from the parliaments of the member states. The number of MEPs contributed by each member state is determined broadly according to national population. The constituency sizes are larger than those for the Westminster Parliament, and so there are fewer MEPs elected in Britain than Westminster MPs (78 as against 646). In each member state the national political parties field candidates, so in Britain the Conservative, Labour and Liberal Democratic parties all field candidates, as do smaller parties. In the European Parliament these members tend to coalesce into quasi-formal political groupings according to ideology, so the socialists will tend to sit together and often vote together on issues, the conservatives do the same and so on.

The European Parliament originally had no legislative powers; its members and committees did no more than give an opinion on policy proposals submitted by the Commission. The Parliament thus constituted simply a forum for general discussion and for criticising proposals. It had the power to summon commissioners before it or before its committees to answer questions concerning policy proposals. It could ask for amendments to proposals, and it could delay the implementation of policies if it wished. The Parliament could dismiss all of the commissioners (though not individuals), something which it has done twice, and it could reject the budget, which it has done on several occasions.

These powers were all that the Parliament had, and without them it would be difficult to justify having a Parliament at all. The reason that it was denied legislative powers is that as all EU law supervenes over national law, a European Parliament with legislative powers would relegate all national legislatures to a secondary status.

However, the process of political integration in the EU, though not vouchsafing the Parliament with legislative powers, has nevertheless increased its importance through the introduction of 'co-decision-making' for most laws. This is where the Council and the Parliament conjointly exercise legislative power. In cases where there is a dispute between the two bodies, then the policy proposal is put before a Conciliation Committee, which is made up of members of the Council and the Parliament in equal numbers. The recommendation of this committee is then put before the Council and the Parliament again for assent.

The European Court of Justice

The Court is located in Luxembourg and its function is to ensure compliance with EU treaties and legislation throughout the member states. The Court will act on a complaint made by the Commission, or occasionally a member state, against another member state, a local authority or a commercial company. Well over 90 per cent of the cases in which the Court intervenes involve commercial companies. A complaint will concern the prima facie violation of EU treaties or laws: for example, the payment of subsidies or levying of taxes proscribed by the treaties, or of monopolistic trading practices or market-sharing agreements etc. The Court also deals with disputes between organisations and their employees over such issues as wrongful dismissal, refusals to promote employees etc. It also acts on disputes between the Commission and the Council.

The Court may be asked for a 'primary ruling' by a judge. The courts of the member states will generally support the ruling if the offender is a company or a local authority. However, given that the member states have executive authority over the EU, there is no mechanism to make a member state comply if it insists on violating a treaty provision. In such cases the matter is normally taken up by the Council and a political compromise is invariably negotiated.

The Court consists of one judge from each member state, plus eight advocates-general, whose principal task is the preparation of draft opinions for the Court.

The decision-making process

Prior to the introduction of co-decision, the decision-making process was thus: the Commission proposed policies, the Parliament advised on them, then the Council authorised these policies, and finally the Commission implemented them. Since the introduction of co-decision, the Council and Parliament authorise policies conjointly.

The policy formation process is deliberately designed to be very open and so is subject to lobbying from governments, commercial companies, trade unions and non-governmental organisations such as environmental groups, consumer protection groups etc. Policies are initiated from within the Council, or the Commission, or by a politician, or a lobby group asking for some issue to be addressed.

The Commission drafts the policy proposal initially, which is then examined by experts in the Commission, in national governments and in the Council. The proposal then goes before the parliamentary committee pertinent to considering such matters (transport, agriculture etc.), whereupon it is presented to the full session of the Parliament, which invariably passes it as it stands, though it may amend it. The proposal then goes to the Council to be authorised or rejected. Since the introduction of co-decision, this authorisation process has been undertaken conjointly with the Parliament. The Council and the Parliament also conjointly decide the Commission's budget, and thus they exercise ultimate executive authority over the Commission. If a policy proposal is a minor issue it will only go to Coreper, which is a body comprising permanent ambassadors from the member states who act on instructions from their national governments.

Without qualified majority voting (QMV) it is very difficult to introduce new policies, as there is likely to be at least one member state which will oppose them. QMV works in the following way: each member state is given a block vote to be used to support or oppose each proposed policy measure. Although the larger states receive a block vote which is larger than that given to the smaller states, the votes are weighted such that the smaller states receive a block disproportionately large relative to their population or GDP. So when there were fifteen member states of the EU, France, Germany, Italy and the

UK were each given a block of ten votes; Spain was given a block of eight; Belgium, Greece, the Netherlands and Portugal were given five each; Austria and Sweden four each; Denmark, Finland and Ireland three each; and Luxembourg two. For a measure to be passed, sixty-two votes out of the total of eighty-seven were required, a threshold of 71 per cent.

Since enlargement, Germany, France, Italy and the UK have each been provided with a block vote of twenty-nine; Poland and Spain have twenty-seven votes each; the Netherlands has thirteen; Belgium, the Czech Republic, Greece, Hungary and Portugal twelve each; Austria and Sweden ten each; Denmark, Ireland, Lithuania, Slovakia and Finland seven each; Cyprus, Estonia, Latvia, Luxembourg and Slovenia four each; and Malta three. This makes a total of 321 votes. A policy measure is assented to if a majority of states (in some cases a two-thirds majority) votes in favour, and there are at least 232 votes in favour (72.3 per cent of the total). Also this should represent at least 62 per cent of the total EU population.

Those issues which are excluded from QMV are common foreign and security policy, taxation, asylum and immigration. Policies regarding such issues require unanimity and thus each nation retains a veto.

If a policy proposal is accepted, it will become either a directive, a regulation or a decision. A directive is a specific policy objective to be implemented throughout the EU, for example uniform safety standards; however, national governments are required to enact legislation via their domestic legislatures to accomplish the specified objective. As legislative time in national legislatures is dominated by the national government's agenda, it is a matter for those national governments to decide whether the directive is a priority and so deserves immediate implementation.

A regulation automatically becomes law throughout the EU immediately it is approved by the Council. Member states are thus obliged to implement such laws through their domestic agencies – the police, the courts etc. This means that a regulation is a much stronger measure than a directive as it bypasses national legislatures.

A decision is a legal measure intended to address a dispute between member states, and usually occurs when an adjudication is required, in other words some compromise deal.

Conclusion

In the sixty years since 1945 Britain has become both better off and worse off. Economically and socially the bulk of the population are much better off. The sectoral shift in the composition of the economy has been determined by a very long-run organically driven change, and has been hindered and then helped by government policy. It has transformed Britain from a bankrupt economy in 1945 to the fourth largest in the world sixty years later. Social policy has meant that the deprivation of the pre-war years has largely been consigned to history.

However, Britain's world status has declined substantially in those sixty years. In 1945 Britain was the third most important global power after the USA and the USSR; today it is not a global power at all. The USA, the EU and China are the hegemonic powers of the present and the foreseeable future, while Britain is marginalised. This is partly due to forces outside Britain's control and partly due to policy. A former US Secretary of State, Dean Acheson, once said that Britain had lost an empire but failed to find a role. Sadly, this remains true today.

Further reading

General

Bartholomew, J. (2006), *The Welfare State We're In*, 2nd edn. London: Politico's.

Burall, S., Donnelly, D. and Weir, S. (eds) (2006), *Not in Our Name: Democracy and Foreign Policy in the UK*. London: Politico's.

Comfort, N. (2005), *The Politics Book*. London: Politico's.

Coxall, B. and Robins, L. (1998), *British Politics since the War*. Basingstoke: Macmillan.

Dearlove, J. and Saunders, P. (2000), *Introduction to British Politics*, 3rd edn. Cambridge: Polity Press.

Dunleavy, P., Gamble, A., Holliday, I. and Peele, G. (eds) (2000), *Developments in British Politics 6*. Basingstoke: Macmillan.

Dunleavy, P., Heffernan, R., Cowley, P. and Hay, C. (eds) (2006), *Developments in British Politics 8*. Basingstoke: Palgrave Macmillan.

Dunleavy, P. and Lawler, P. (eds) (2000), *New Labour in Power*. Manchester: Manchester University Press.

Edwards, G. (2006), *British Politics Unravelled*. London: Politico's.

Jessop, B. (1992), 'From Social Democracy to Thatcherism: Twenty-Five Years of British Politics', in Abercombie, N. and Warde, A. (eds), *Social Change in Contemporary Britain*. Cambridge: Polity Press.

Kavanagh, D. (1996), *British Politics: Continuities and Change*, 3rd edn. Oxford: Oxford University Press.

Kavanagh, D. (1997), *The Reordering of British Politics: Politics after Thatcher*. Oxford: Oxford University Press.

Kavanagh, D. and Morris, P. (1994), *Consensus Politics from Attlee to Major*, 2nd edn. Oxford: Blackwell.

McIntosh, R. (2006), *Challenge to Democracy: Politics, Trade Union Power and Economic Failure 1973–77*. London: Politico's.

Marsh, D. and Rhodes, R. (1992), *Implementing Thatcherite Policies: Audit of an Era*. Buckingham: Open University Press.

Chapter 1

Coxall, B. and Robins, L. (1998), *British Politics since the War*. Basingstoke: Macmillan, ch. 1.

Eccleshall, R. and Walker, G. (eds) (1998), *Biographical Dictionary of British Prime Ministers*. London: Routledge.

Ellis, R. and Treasure, G. (2005), *Britain's Prime Ministers: From Walpole to Thatcher*. London: Shepheard-Walwyn.

Hennessy, P. (2000), *The Prime Minister: The Office and Its Holders since 1945*. London: Allen Lane.

Chapter 2

Blackburn, R. (2006), *King and Country: Monarchy and the Future King Charles III*. London: Politico's.

Dearlove, J. and Saunders, P. (2000), *Introduction to British Politics*, 3rd edn. Cambridge: Polity Press, ch. 2, 7, 9 & 11.

Dunleavy, P., Heffernan R., Cowley, P. and Hay, C. (eds) (2006), *Developments in British Politics 8*. Basingstoke: Palgrave Macmillan, ch. 2, 3 & 7.

Hennessy, P. (1995), *The Hidden Wiring: Unearthing the British Constitution*. London: Victor Gollancz.

Kavanagh, D. (1996), *British Politics: Continuities and Change*, 3rd edn. Oxford. Oxford University Press, ch. 3, 10–13 & 15.

Punnett, R. (1994), *British Government and Politics*, 6th edn. Aldershot: Dartmouth, ch. 6–11.

Richardson, J. (1979), *Governing under Pressure*. Oxford: Martin Robertson.

Chapter 3

Butcher, H. (1990), *Local Government and Thatcherism*. London: Routledge.

Dearlove, J. (1979), *The Reorganisation of British Local Government*. London: Cambridge University Press.

Dearlove, J. and Saunders, P. (2000), *Introduction to British Politics*, 3rd edn. Cambridge: Polity Press, ch. 8.

Dunleavy, P., Heffernan R., Cowley, P. and Hay, C. (eds) (2006), *Developments in British Politics 8*. Basingstoke: Palgrave Macmillan, ch. 8.

Jones, B. and Kavanagh, D. (2003), *British Politics Today*. Manchester: Manchester University Press, ch. 14.

Pilkington, C. (2002), *Devolution in Britain Today*. Manchester: Manchester University Press.

Punnett, R. (1994), *British Government and Politics*, 6th edn. Aldershot: Dartmouth, ch. 13 & 14.

Stevens, A. (forthcoming), *Local Government*. London: Politico's.

Chapter 4

Cowley, P. (2006), *The Rebels: How Blair Mislaid His Majority*. London: Politico's.

Coxall, B. and Robins, L. (1998), *British Politics since the War*. Basingstoke: Macmillan, ch. 7.

Dearlove, J. and Saunders, P. (2000), *Introduction to British Politics*, 3rd edn. Cambridge: Polity Press, ch. 3.

Devigne, R. (1994), *Recasting Conservatism*. New Haven and London: Yale University Press.

Dunleavy, P., Heffernan R., Cowley, P. and Hay, C. (eds) (2006), *Developments in British Politics 8*. Basingstoke: Palgrave Macmillan, ch. 1, 4 & 16.

Heywood, A. (1998), *Political Ideologies: An Introduction*. Basingstoke: Macmillan.

Kavanagh, D. (1996), *British Politics: Continuities and Change*, 3rd edn. Oxford. Oxford University Press, ch. 7.

Leach, R. (2002), *Political Ideology in Britain*. Basingstoke: Palgrave.

Philp, C. (ed.) (2006), *Conservative Revival: Blueprint for a Better Britain*. London: Politico's.

Rosen, G. (2005), *Old Labour to New: The Dreams That Inspired, the Battles That Divided*. London: Politico's.

Chapter 5

Dearlove, J. and Saunders, P. (2000), *Introduction to British Politics*, 3rd edn. Cambridge: Polity Press, ch. 12.

Froyen, R. (2002), *Macroeconomics: Theories and Policies*, 7th edn. Upper Saddle River, NJ: Prentice Hall.

Grant, W. (2002), *Economic Policy in Britain*. Basingstoke: Macmillan, ch. 1, 3–6 & 8.

Marquand, D. and Seldon, A. (eds) (1996), *The Ideas That Shaped Post-War Britain*. London: Fontana, ch. 3 and 4.

Skidelsky, R. (1979), 'The Decline of Keynesian Politics', in Crouch, C. (ed.), *State and Society in Contemporary Capitalism*. London: Croom Helm.

Smith, D. (1987), *The Rise and Fall of Monetarism*. Harmondsworth: Penguin.

Chapter 6

Atkinson, A. (1983), *The Economics of Inequality*, 2nd edn. Oxford: Oxford University Press.

Culyer, A. J. (1980), *The Political Economy of Social Policy*. Oxford: Martin Robertson.

Dilnot, A. and Walker, I. (eds) (1989), *The Economics of Social Security*. Oxford: Oxford University Press, ch. 9, 10, 13 & 14.

Dunleavy, P., Gamble, A., Holliday, I. and Peele, G. (eds) (2000), *Developments in British Politics 6*. Basingstoke: Macmillan, ch. 14.

Johnson, P. and Stark, G. (1989), *Taxation and Social Security 1979–1989: The Impact on Household Incomes*. London: Institute for Fiscal Studies.

Stiglitz, J. (1988), *The Economics of the Public Sector*, 2nd edn. New York: W. W. Norton.

Chapter 7

Barr, N. (1998), *Economics of the Welfare State*, 3rd edn. Oxford: Oxford University Press, ch. 12.

Barr, N. and Whynes, D. (eds) (1993), *Current Issues in the Economics of Welfare*. Basingstoke: Macmillan, ch. 8.

Coxall, B. and Robins, L. (1998), *British Politics since the War*. Basingstoke: Macmillan, ch. 10.

Culyer, A., Maynard, A. and Posnett, J. (1990), *Competition in Health Care: Reforming the NHS*. London: Macmillan, ch. 1–3, 5 & 9.

Dearlove, J. and Saunders, P. (2000), *Introduction to British Politics*, 3rd edn. Cambridge: Polity Press, ch. 13.

Dunleavy, P., Heffernan R., Cowley, P. and Hay, C. (eds) (2006), *Developments in British Politics 8*. Basingstoke: Palgrave Macmillan, ch. 15.

Glennerster, H. (1995), *British Social Policy since 1945*. Oxford: Blackwell.

Le Grand, J. and Bartlett, W. (eds) (1993), *Quasi-Markets and Social Policy*. London: Macmillan, ch. 4.

Chapter 8

Barr, N. (1998), *Economics of the Welfare State*, 3rd edn. Oxford: Oxford University Press, ch. 13.

Barr, N. and Whynes, D. (eds) (1993), *Current Issues in the Economics of Welfare*. Basingstoke: Macmillan, ch. 9.

Coxall, B. and Robins, L. (1998), *British Politics since the War*. Basingstoke: Macmillan, ch. 10.

Dearlove, J. and Saunders, P. (2000), *Introduction to British Politics*, 3rd edn. Cambridge: Polity Press, ch. 13.

Dunleavy, P., Heffernan R., Cowley, P. and Hay, C. (eds) (2006), *Developments in British Politics 8*. Basingstoke: Palgrave Macmillan, ch. 15.

Glennerster, H. (1995), *British Social Policy since 1945*. Oxford: Blackwell.

Johnes, G. (1993), *The Economics of Education*. Basingstoke: Macmillan, ch. 5 & 7–9.

Le Grand, J. and Bartlett, W. (eds) (1993), *Quasi-Markets and Social Policy*. London: Macmillan, ch. 6.

Chapter 9

Barr, N. (1998), *Economics of the Welfare State*, 3rd edn. Oxford: Oxford University Press, ch. 14.

Barr, N. and Whynes, D. (eds) (1993), *Current Issues in the Economics of Welfare*. Basingstoke: Macmillan, ch. 10.

Harvey, J. (2000), *Urban Land Economics*, 5th edn. Basingstoke: Macmillan, ch. 18.

Le Grand, J. and Bartlett, W. (eds) (1993), *Quasi-Markets and Social Policy*. London: Macmillan, ch. 7.

Malpass, P. and Murie, A. (1994), *Housing Policy and Practice*, 4th edn. London: Macmillan.

Whitehead, C. and Kleinman, M. (1987), *Private Rented Housing in the 1980s and 1990s*. Cambridge: Granta.

Chapter 10

Banister, D. (1994), *Transport Planning in the UK, USA and Europe*. London. E. & F. N. Spon.

British Railways Board (1963), *The Reshaping of British Railways (the Beeching Report)*. London: HMSO.

Developing an Integrated Transport Policy (1997). Department of the Environment, Transport and the Regions.

Glaister, S., Burnham, J., Stevens, H. and Travers, T. (1998), *Transport Policy in Britain*. London: Macmillan.

Glaister S. and Travers, T. (1997), 'Governing the Underground: Funding, Management and Democracy for London's Tube', in *Public Transport on the Move: A Policy Review*. Bath: Centre for the Study of Regulated Industries.

Gwilliam, K. (1964), *Transport and Public Policy*. London: George Allen & Unwin.

Standing Advisory Committee on Trunk Road Assessment (1994), *Trunk Roads and the Generation of Traffic*. London: HMSO.

Transport Ten Year Plan 2000 (2000). Department of the Environment, Transport and the Regions.

Chapter 11

Bacon R. and Eltis, W. (1978), *Britain's Economic Problem: Too Few Producers*, 2nd edn. London: Macmillan.

Bacon R. and Eltis, W. (1996), *Britain's Economic Problem Revisited*. Basingstoke: Macmillan.

Coxall, B. and Robins, L. (1998), *British Politics since the War*. Basingstoke: Macmillan, ch. 9.

Dearlove, J. and Saunders, P. (2000), *Introduction to British Politics*, 3rd edn. Cambridge: Polity Press, ch. 12.

Punnett, R. (1994), *British Government and Politics*, 6th edn. Aldershot: Dartmouth, ch. 12.

Saunders, P. and Harris, C. (1994), *Privatisation and Popular Capitalism*. Buckingham: Open University Press.

Chapter 12

Baylis, J. (1984), *Anglo-American Defence Relations 1939–84: The Special Relationship*, 2nd edn. London: Macmillan.

Byrd, P. (ed.) (1988), *British Foreign Policy under Thatcher*. Oxford: Phillip Allan.

Carver, M. (1992), *Tightrope Walking: British Defence Policy since 1945*. London: Hutchinson.

Coxall, B. and Robins, L. (1998), *British Politics since the War*. Basingstoke: Macmillan, ch. 11.

Dunleavy, P., Heffernan R., Cowley, P. and Hay, C. (eds) (2006), *Developments in British Politics 8*. Basingstoke: Palgrave Macmillan, ch. 10.

Little, R. and Wickham-Jones, M. (eds) (2000), *New Labour's Foreign Policy*. Manchester: Manchester University Press.

Vital, D. (1968), *The Making of British Foreign Policy*. London: Allen & Unwin.

Chapter 13

Anderson, E. and O'Neil, T. (2006), *A New Equity Agenda?: Reflections on the 2006 World Development Report, the 2005 Human Development Report and the 2005 Report on the World Social Situation*. London: Overseas Development

Institute.

Bowers, J. (1997), *Sustainability and Environmental Economics: An Alternative Text*. Harlow: Longman.

Budge, I. (2004), *The New British Politics*, 3rd edn. Harlow: Pearson Longman, ch. 23.

Department of the Environment (1990), *This Common Inheritance*, Cm 1200.

Department of the Environment, Transport and the Regions (1999), *The UK Environment*. London: HMSO.

Dunleavy, P., Gamble, A., Holliday, I. and Peele, G. (eds) (2000), *Developments in British Politics 6*. Basingstoke: Macmillan, ch. 15.

Jerker, E. and Hatashima, H. (1993), *The Inter-Country Distribution of UK Overseas Development Assistance*. Brighton: Institute of Development Studies.

May, R. (1985), *Overseas development aid and the British domestic economy – a micro-economic study*.

Ministry of Overseas Development (1975), *Overseas Development: The Changing Emphasis in British Aid Policies: More Help for the Poorest*, Cmnd 6270.

Chapter 14

Coxall, B. and Robins, L. (1998), *British Politics since the War*. Basingstoke: Macmillan, ch. 5.

Dearlove, J. and Saunders, P. (2000), *Introduction to British Politics*, 3rd edn. Cambridge: Polity Press, ch. 16.

George, S. (1998), *An Awkward Partner: Britain and the European Community*, 3rd edn. Oxford: Oxford University Press.

Kavanagh, D. (1996), *British Politics: Continuities and Change*, 3rd edn. Oxford: Oxford University Press, ch. 4.

Punnett, R. (1994), *British Government and Politics*, 6th edn. Aldershot: Dartmouth, ch. 14.

Sawyer, M. (ed.) (2005), *The UK Economy*. Oxford: Oxford University Press, ch. 3.

Index

unemployment 57, 62–3, 63, 69, 73, 79, 138
benefits 76–7, 80–1
unilateral nuclear disarmament 150
United Nations 59
universities 100–3
  see also Cambridge University; Open University; Oxford University; Scotland universities; Wales universities
unsecured credit 113–14
unwritten constitution 17
upper house *see* House of Lords
urban districts 20
USA
  aid budget 163
  airlines 125
  atomic bomb 147
  Blair environmental policies 167
  capitalism 174
  defence 95, 145, 147, 169
  economic power 148
  foreign direct investment 138
  foreign policy 146–7
  global warming 166
  governance 7
  hegemonic power 58–60, 147, 151, 154, 174–5, 183
  influence 151
  intelligence information 151
  inter-continental ballistic missiles (ICBM) 149
  see also Polaris
  partial withdrawal from Europe 175
  post-war cooperation 146
  productivity 144
  Skybolt 149
  Suez crisis 169
USSR
  Chernobyl 157
  collapse of 152, 154, 175
  communism 174
  Egypt 148

Korea 146
photographic sortie over 149
post-war threat 145
utilities (gas, electricity and water) 21–2, 134–5, 139–40
  privatisation 134–5, 140

V-bombers 147, 149
V/STOL (vertical/short take-off and landing) 151
Vickers Valiant 147
Victoria line 119
Vietnam War 150
vocational education 100–1
voluntary work 79
voters **45**, 47

wage councils 141–2
Wales
  devolution 7, 27–9, 32–3
  Secretary of State for 29
  universities 102
Wall Street crash (1929) 37, 54
Walters, Alan 5, 71
war-time coalition government 36–7
warship production 150
Waterloo 121
wave power 162
welfare
  payments 83
  state 2, 76–7, 95
  to work 83
Welsh Assembly 27–9, 119
Welwyn Garden City (1920) 105
West Germany
  aid budget 163
  British Army of the Rhine 146
  defence 146, 176
  economy 169, 172, 174
  European unification 175
  foreign and defence policy 174
  industry 129
  manufacturing industry 130
West Lothian question 29